ANCIENT

**COVER**
Limestone head of a bearded man. Cypro-Archaic. Given by Professor R. G. Collingwood from the collection of John Ruskin. Ht. 0·298 [1938.347].

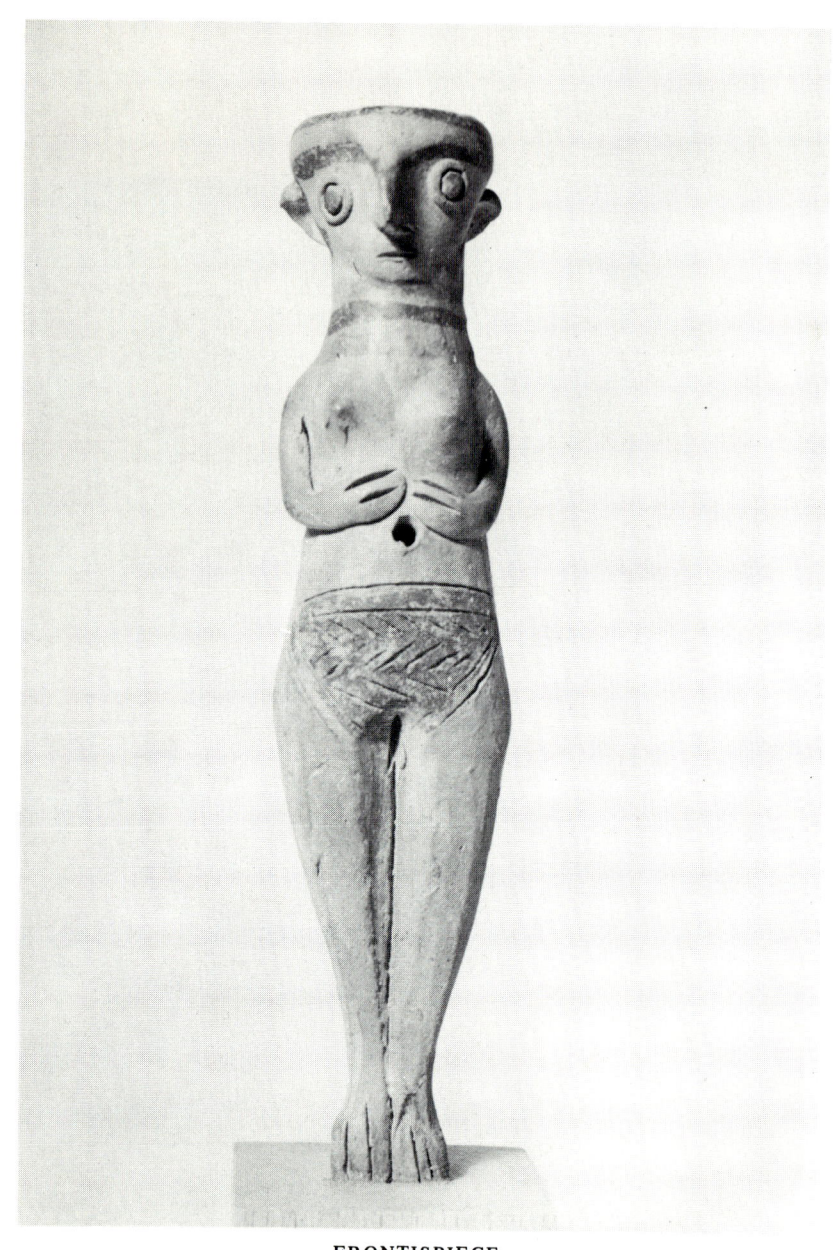

FRONTISPIECE
Terracotta statuette of a naked woman, details in black and red paint. Late Cypriot II. From *Ayia Paraskevi*, Nicosia, from the collection of M. Ohnefalsch-Richter. Ht. 0·204 [1896.2].

UNIVERSITY OF OXFORD
ASHMOLEAN MUSEUM

# ANCIENT CYPRUS

BY

A. C. BROWN
(Ashmolean Museum)

AND

H. W. CATLING
(British School at Athens)

OXFORD

PRINTED FOR THE VISITORS

AND SOLD AT THE ASHMOLEAN MUSEUM

1975

Text and illustrations
© the Ashmolean Museum 1975

ISBN 0 9000 9018 9

OTHER TITLES IN THIS SERIES
Ancient Egypt
Archaeology, Artefacts and the Bible

Set in Photon Times and
Printed in Great Britain at the Alden Press, Oxford

# Preface

The Department exhibits perhaps the most representative collection of Cypriot antiquities to be seen outside the island. Ruskin, Myres, Collingwood and Schaeffer have been among those who helped to found and augment it. I commend this booklet not only as a guide to the exhibition, but also as a concise introduction to a field of study in which those associated with the Ashmolean have figured prominently.

HUMPHREY CASE
Keeper,
Department of Antiquities.

May 1974

# Acknowledgements

We are most grateful to Dr. V. Karageorghis and his colleagues for every assistance in Cyprus; to two successive Keepers of the Department of Antiquities, Mr. R. W. Hamilton and Mr. H. J. Case, and to many of our colleagues there and in the Heberden Coin Room, for help and encouragement. Mrs. Pat Clarke drew the maps and diagrams and Miss O. M. Godwin and the staff of the Ashmolean's photographic studio prepared the other illustrations.

# Contents

| | | |
|---|---|---|
| | PREFACE | v |
| | ACKNOWLEDGEMENTS | vi |
| | NOTES | viii |
| | CHRONOLOGICAL TABLE | ix |
| | INTRODUCTION | 1 |
| I | The Neolithic and Chalcolithic Periods | 8 |
| II | The Bronze Age; The Early, Middle and Late Cypriot Periods | 12 |
| III | The Iron Age; The Cypro-Geometric, Archaic and Classic Periods | 37 |
| IV | Hellenistic and Roman Cyprus | 63 |
| V | Early Christian, Byzantine, Medieval and Later Cyprus | 71 |
| | SELECT BIBLIOGRAPHY | 80 |
| | INDEX OF EXCAVATED MATERIAL FROM CYPRUS IN THE ASHMOLEAN MUSEUM | 83 |

# Notes

1. Although the following account is as comprehensive as possible within obvious limitations of space, it is necessarily biased towards the Ashmolean collection of Cypriot Antiquities.

2. The numbers which appear in brackets in the captions are the serial numbers of the objects in the accessions registers of the Department of Antiquities.

3. Measurements are expressed in metres or parts of a metre. The following abbreviations are used in references to dimensions: Ht. Height; L. Length; D. Diameter.

4. The spelling of place-names follows as far as possible that used in the Survey of Cyprus Administration and Road Map.

# Chronological Table
(BC dates are approximate)

|  |  |  |  |
|---|---|---|---|
| Neolithic | I | 5800–5250 | |
| | II | 3500–3000 | |
| Chalcolithic | I | 3000–2500 | |
| | II | 2500–2300 | |
| Early Cypriot | I | 2300–2200 | |
| | II | 2200–2100 | |
| | III | 2100–2000 | |
| Middle Cypriot | | 2000–1600 | |
| Late Cypriot | I | 1600–1400 | |
| | II | 1400–1200 | |
| | III | 1200–1050 | |
| Cypro-Geometric | I | 1050– 950 | (Early Iron Age c. 1050–900) |
| | II | 950– 850 | (Middle Iron Age I 900–725) |
| | III | 850– 700 | (Middle Iron Age II 725–600) |
| Cypro-Archaic | I | 700– 600 | |
| | II | 600– 475 | (Late Iron Age c. 600—Hellenistic) |
| Cypro-Classic | I | 475– 325 | |
| Hellenistic | | 325– 50 | |
| Roman | | 50 BC–AD 395 | |
| Byzantine | | AD 395–1191 | |
| (Isaac Comnenus, Emperor of Cyprus | | 1184–1191) | |
| (Richard I of England, Lord of Cyprus | | 1191–1192) | |
| Lusignan Dynasty | | 1192–1489 | |
| Venetian | | 1489–1571 | |
| Turkish | | 1571–1878 | |

*Note.* Archaeologists conventionally divide Cypriot prehistory into a series of major phases approximating to technological stages: Neolithic, Chalcolithic, Bronze and Iron Ages. This traditional 19th-century terminology is slowly being modified, 'Cypriot' now regularly replaces 'Bronze' in the Early, Middle and Late Bronze Age. For the early periods Neolithic to the Middle Cypriot the table above follows H.-G, Buchholz and V. Karageorghis, *Prehistoric Greece and Cyprus* (1973), the current views on Minoan chronology are therefore taken into account, but this is at variance with the chronological scheme of many Cypriot archaeologists. The dating of the Later Bronze Age and the Iron Age follows, for the most part, that set out in the various volumes of the *Swedish Cyprus Expedition*. For the Iron Age the Swedes devised a terminology, essentially to describe changing pottery styles, akin to that used for these periods in Mainland Greece, thus Cypro-Geometric, -Archaic, -Classic. A modification of these divisions has been suggested by J. Birmingham, 'The Chronology of Some Early and Middle Iron Age Sites' in *American Journal of Archaeology* **67** (1963). These are noted above, although the Swedish terminology has been followed in the text.

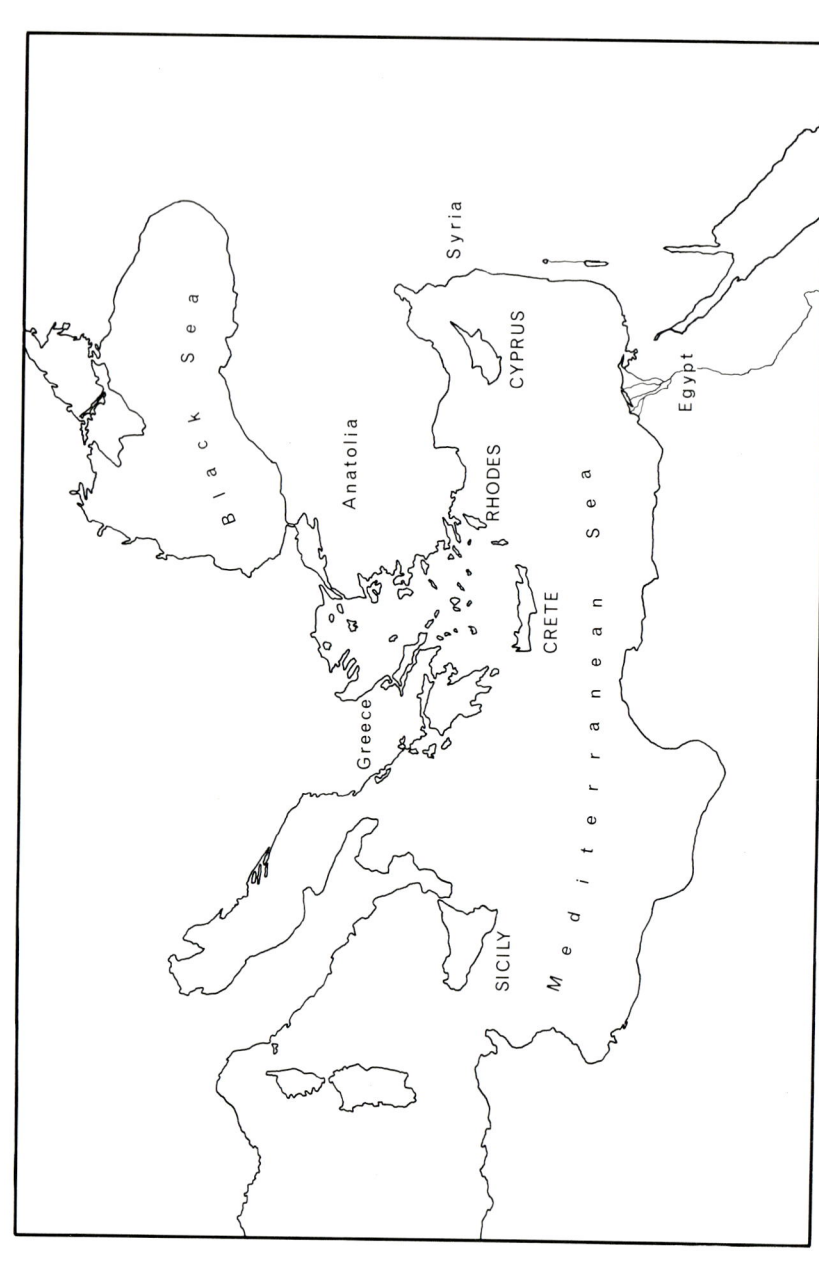

# Introduction

## THE ASHMOLEAN COLLECTION

The remains of nearly 8,000 years of human history lie in the soil of Cyprus, remains that have stimulated the interest and curiosity of historians and archaeologists for over a hundred years.

The most famous of the early collectors of Cypriot antiquities was General Luigi Palma di Cesnola, an Italian-American who had served successfully in the wars of 1848 in Austria, the Crimean War and The American Civil War before being appointed American consul in Larnaka in 1865, at the age of 33. He was to hold simultaneously the post of Russian consul.

For the next 12 years Cesnola spent much of his time exploring ancient sites on the island and amassing a vast collection of antiquities. The story is entertainingly told by Cesnola himself in *Cyprus, its Ancient Cities, Tombs and Temples* (1877), how as American consul he was forbidden by the Turkish rulers of Cyprus to export his collection, but as Russian consul he contrived to remove the greater part to London in 1872. He sold some objects to museums and private collectors, including General Pitt-Rivers, and some of these antiquities are now in the Pitt Rivers Museum, Oxford. The bulk of the collection was sold to the Metropolitan Museum of Art, New York. Previously John Ruskin, Slade Professor of Art at Oxford, had visited the antiquities when they were temporarily exhibited in London and probably met Cesnola himself. He was deeply distressed by the sale to America, and was later to write that the collection had been '... offered for an old song to the British Museum and the authorities (my own impression is through pure and mere jealousy) offered an older song for [it], and let it be bought over their heads by New York, where doubtless the enlightened public will soon break it all up for soft building materials'. His disgust at the apathy of the British authorities and the deep impression which the Cypriot antiquities had made on him led Ruskin about 2 years later to give Cesnola £1,000 to pursue his 'researches'. He received in return a number of antiquities of various sorts, some of which passed direct to the University. Others, sent by Cesnola to Ruskin, were long afterwards given to the Ashmolean by Professor R. G. Collingwood, whose father had been Ruskin's secretary and biographer. Though the Ruskin episode seems a minor one in the Cesnola story, it marked the beginning of Oxford's interest in Cyprus.

The Cypriot gallery in the Ashmolean is called the 'Myres Room' after Sir John Linton Myres, Wykeham Professor of Ancient History at Oxford (1910–1939), who went out to Cyprus as a young man in 1894. He was first attached to the British Museum's excavations at Amathus, and later in the year he excavated for the Cyprus Exploration Fund, which had been formed to channel the growing interest in Cypriot archaeology. He was the first to dig in Cyprus to reconstruct the history of the island, rather than to find museum-worthy objects. Myres gave his share of the finds to the University of Oxford where it now forms the nucleus of the Ashmolean's Cypriot collection. The Index of Excavated Material (p. 83) gives details of the sites from which his finds came, and of other Cypriot excavations either promoted directly by the Ashmolean or by closely associated authorities. In a *Catalogue of the Cyprus Museum* (1899), Myres, in collaboration with the German archaeologist Max Ohnefalsch-Richter, for the first time attempted to present an orderly account of the material civilisation of Cyprus in relation to events in neighbouring regions, and so make possible a framework of absolute chronology.

Myres revised and improved this fundamental work in 1914, when he published the *Handbook of the Cesnola Collection of Antiquities from Cyprus* (the Metropolitan Museum of Art, New York). In the introduction to his handbook, he wrote that in 1865, when Cesnola was appointed consul 'the moment certainly was near when Cyprus must be won for archaeology, and "digging" be transformed from a mischievous pastime into a weapon of historical science'. This transformation had been achieved by Myres himself. Though not directly involved in Cypriot archaeology after 1913, he acted in an advisory capacity in drafting a new Antiquities Law under the British administration of the island, and in setting up the Department of Antiquities which was established in 1935.

Since 1935 this Department has been responsible for many of the most important excavations carried out on the island and the results

## INTRODUCTION

are published not only in the *Report of the Department of Antiquities, Cyprus* but also in a number of monographs on individual sites. The Ashmolean has received objects from some of these excavations and from excavations carried out by foreign missions on the island, notably the French mission under Professor C. F. A. Schaeffer at Enkomi.

Foreign archaeological missions have had a profound effect on the development of Cypriot archaeology, none greater than the Swedish Cyprus expedition of 1927–1931 which, under its leader Professor Einar Gjerstad, undertook a series of excavations at sites of all periods from Neolithic to Late Roman, reporting the results in a series of volumes—*Swedish Cyprus Expedition* I–IV (1934–1972)—which forms one of the main foundations of Cypriot scholarship.

The Ashmolean has taken great interest in Cypriot field archaeology both by mounting its own expeditions and by supporting excavations otherwise sponsored. It has in many cases received in return a share of the finds, a process which began with Myres and continues to the present day (see Index of Excavated Material, p. 83). In addition to material from excavations the Museum has acquired many objects, both by gift and purchase, of whose find circumstances naturally much less is known. There is also a large study collection of pottery fragments assembled from sites throught the island.

## GEOGRAPHICAL POSITION

Cyprus lies tucked in at the eastern end of the Mediterranean Sea, the third largest of its islands. The Syro-Palestinian coast is little more than 50 miles away to the east, and in clear weather the southern mountains of Turkey can be seen across the water from the northern shore. To the south, Egypt is a relatively close neighbour. Greece and the Islands of the Aegean are easily accessible to the west. So it is no surprise that the island's history reflects the fortunes of her more powerful neighbours. Inevitably as a bridgehead between Europe and Asia, Cyprus became involved, in a seemingly unending process, in the struggle for political and economic domination. This involvement is well illustrated by the ambivalent nature of the island's material culture; in part it is European, in part Asiatic. But always the amalgam is completed and given individuality by a third element, that of Cyprus herself.

The areas of human settlement have always been closely related to the physical features of the island. There are two dominant mountain systems. In the north the Kyrenia range runs parallel to the coast for about 60 miles; it is relatively well watered and the narrow plain between its foothills and the sea is very fertile. This strip of land attracted some of the island's earliest hunters and farmers. The greater part of western and central Cyprus is occupied by the Troodos mountain range. Copper ores are found on its northern and eastern slopes. These ores were easily extracted and have been exploited since the Early Cypriot period (the Early Bronze Age). Along the south-west coast is a succession of torrent beds, full only in the rainy season, which drain the massif by cutting through the foothills to the sea. Here, on the terraces of these rivers, early settlers found very favourable conditions for both hunting and farming.

Between the Kyrenia and Troodos ranges there is a wide plain, very fertile in parts, which crosses the island from north-west to south-east. It may once have been forested, but apart from its citrus groves, it is now treeless. The western part of the plain between Nicosia and Morphou Bay is drained by a number of watercourses and seems to have been quite densely populated even during the Early Cypriot period. The eastern section from Nicosia to Salamis Bay may have been more heavily wooded, for fewer sites have been found there.

Only at Famagusta are there now deep water berths for modern ships. A number of river mouths and deep inlets that made fine ports in antiquity have long since silted up. Ancient ships, too, would have been well enough served by the small coves and beaches of the exposed north coast and by the beaches of the more sheltered south coast. We are reminded of early Cypriot seafaring by a little clay model of a boat, now in Paris, datable to the Middle Bronze Age, with eight sailors on board.

Internal communications in much of Cyprus have always been reasonably good, except between the far west and the rest of the island. Easy passes give access from the north coast through the Kyrenia mountains to the central plain. The plain itself offered no real obstacles to travellers; pack animals (pl. IV), carts and even chariots could have been used here without trouble. Travellers in

# INTRODUCTION

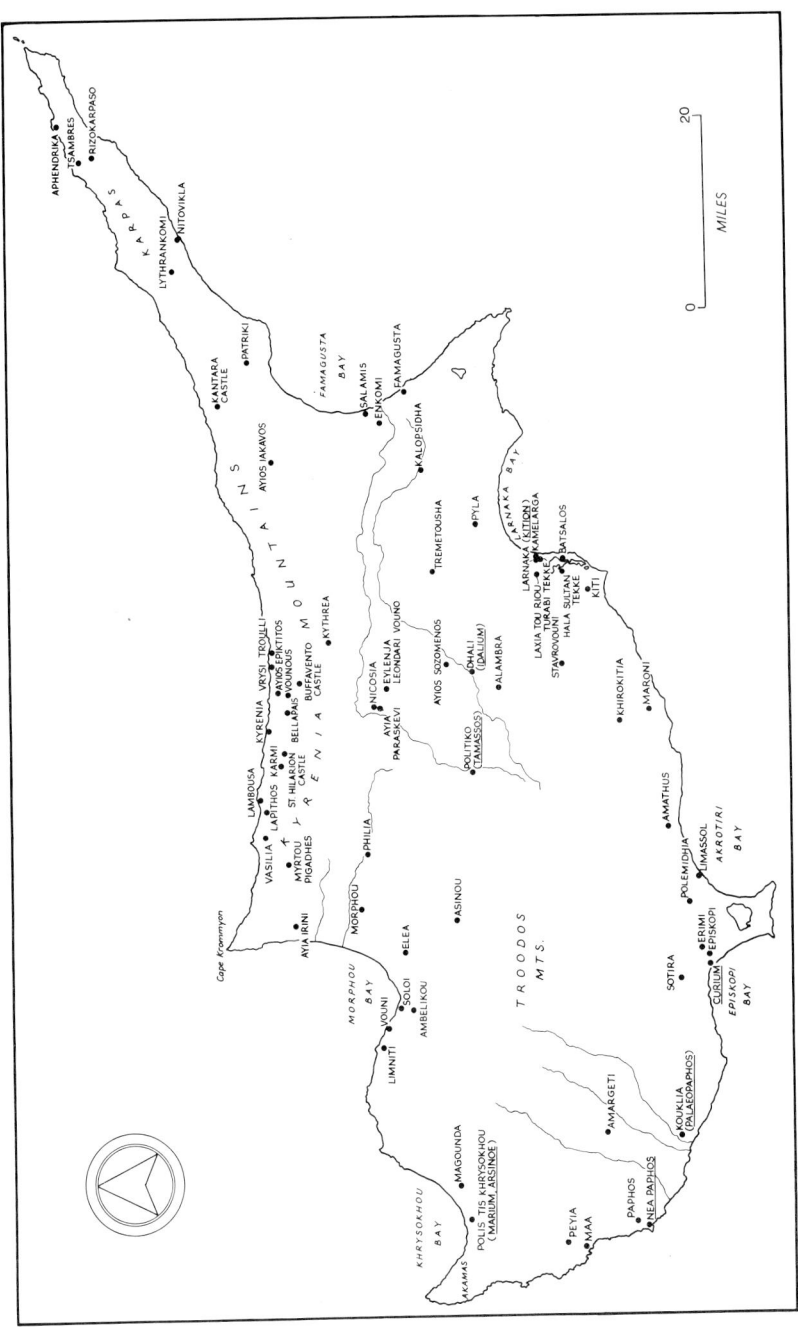

Cyprus from Strabo in Roman times through the Middle Ages, when pilgrims chronicled their visits, journeyed from city to city throughout the island. They complained of the heat, of the risk of fever, of the obstinacy of their mules, but very seldom of difficult terrain.

## SOURCES AND CHRONOLOGY

Before the regular survival of written records, the development of human settlement and civilisation in Cyprus can only be reconstructed piecemeal from archaeological evidence; long after the first written records, archaeology also provides vital supplementary information.

Unlike Anatolia, Palestine or Mesopotamia, the remains of human settlements in Cyprus do not form conspicuous artificial mounds, or *tells* (such as Tell es Sultan, at Jericho), whose stratified deposits and their contents, properly excavated and correctly interpreted, may offer an almost uninterrupted record of human activity from the earliest times to the present. Although some *areas* in Cyprus were continuously occupied over a long period, the actual sites changed location and no long sequence of settlement was built up on any one of them. When Sir John Myres formulated his pioneer scheme for the relative chronology of prehistoric Cyprus, by far the greater part of the evidence consisted of pottery and small finds from cemeteries. His method was to establish a sequence of pottery styles, using better known foreign imports as a guide to the sequence and to establish absolute dates. The scheme which he devised is continually being revised and adapted to take account of recent finds, yet it still remains workable; in recent years, the absolute dating of the earliest periods of human settlement has come to depend on Carbon 14.

In Cyprus, as in other parts of the Old World, historical dates are not applicable before about 2000 BC. Approximations of the absolute ages of earlier events depend on radiocarbon dating. Basically this method consists in measuring the residual level of activity of the radioactive carbon (C-14) in organic substances such as charcoal. The experimental uncertainty in the method used is expressed as a standard deviation (thus $3875 \text{ bc} \pm 145$) which implies that there is about a 66% chance that the true age of the sample lay within the limits expressed (4020–3730 bc) and about

## INTRODUCTION

95% chance that it lay within twice these limits (4165–3585 bc). Naturally too the usefulness of a particular determination for archaeological or historical purposes depends on the degree of certainty with which the sample can be associated with well-defined cultural stages. (The notation bc instead of BC indicates that a date has been obtained by radiocarbon.)

The earliest foreign pottery found in Cyprus comes from Syria, and is dated to the third millennium BC; a little Minoan pottery from Crete can be dated to the first half of the second millennium. Increasing quantities of Mycenaean pottery from Greece reached the island during the second half of the second millennium. Imported artefacts continue to provide a rough-and-ready measure of passing time well into the first millennium, when Cyprus became successively involved in the military and diplomatic activities of Egypt, Assyria and Persia, which were recorded either in contemporary royal annals or later by classical historians. Of the early geographers, Strabo was one of the first actually to visit Cyprus; he completed his *Geographica* about AD 23 and describes the island in the fourteenth book, 'in excellence it falls behind no one of the islands, for it is rich in wine and oil, and uses home-grown wheat. There are mines of copper in plenty . . .'.

# I. The Neolithic And Chalcolithic Periods

The first settlers in Cyprus arrived not long after 6000 BC and established themselves at a number of widely separated coastal and inland sites. They were farmers and hunters, attracted by fertile land and perennial springs. Their well-developed and distinctive culture is called 'Neolithic I'. The best-known site of this period is the partly excavated settlement of Khirokitia in southern Cyprus.

Flint sickle blades and stone querns found on the site show that grain was harvested and ground into flour; sheep and goat bones suggest that animals may have been domesticated; flint arrowheads and the antlers of deer and moufflon (wild sheep) prove that hunting supplemented the meat supply. Fragments of obsidian have been found, which analysis indicates may have come from the Çiftlik area of Turkey, thus suggesting contact, albeit sporadic, between Cyprus and the outside world.

The settlers lived in round huts, built with stone walls and roofed with domes of mud bricks. The dead were buried under the hut floors in small pit-graves. The fine-grained stone bowl (pl. Ia) is typical of the vessels, some of considerable size, which have been found on the site. The use of pottery was almost unknown during the Neolithic I period.

These early settlements seem to have been abandoned by about 5000 BC, and until the arrival about 3500 BC of a new group of settlers, Neolithic II, the history of the island is obscure. The gap of over a thousand years between the abandonment of the earliest sites and the building of the Neolithic II settlement of Sotira may perhaps be narrowed by finds from the site of Troulli and more recent excavations. The excavators at Troulli, on the north coast of Cyprus near Kyrenia, found stone vases characteristic of Neolithic I, but no pottery in the earliest levels, and a distinctive type of pottery with a lustrous slip decorated with reserved panels and circles (pl. Ib) in the later levels. In the absence of a Carbon 14 date for Troulli, the dating of the site is very uncertain. Currently another settlement nearby, at Ayios Epiktitos, *Vrysi* is being

Plate I: a. Stone spouted bowl. Neolithic. Perhaps from Khirokitia. L. 0.136 [1954.4]. b. Fragments of Red-on-White ware bowls, decorated with circles and lines from Troulli, and with 'combed' patterns from Sotira. Neolithic. Ht. of largest sherd 0.055.

investigated, where a date has been obtained from hearth material in one of the houses, 3875 bc±145 (Brm-182). The settlement, which shows evidence of occupation over a long period, consists of stone-built houses of irregular plan, densely packed together in groups on a narrow, windy, headland; paved passageways separated the groups. Some of the buildings seem to have been partially subterranean. Although the house walls were thin, some still stand to a height of 3 metres. Inside, the houses were equipped with stone benches and containers built of upright stones; often there was a large circular hearth on the floor. The houses were also used as workshops for bone working and the making of stone axes and chisels. Much pottery has been found, painted with a variety of patterns (pl. II). As at Khirokitia, the settlers were farmers and hunters. Behind the settlement lay fertile land between the Kyrenia foothills and the sea; evidence of wheat, barley, lentils, grapes and olives has all been found in the settlement. It seems from the Carbon 14 date that this community flourished between the abandonment of Khirokitia and the arrival of the Neolithic II people.

It is probable that these newcomers who built villages mainly along the south coast, came from outside the island: links with south Palestine have been suggested. One of the settlements, on a hill-top at Sotira, near Episkopi, has been excavated. In it was found a series of closely packed houses of various shapes, built partly of stone, partly of mud brick, each with its own hearth. The dead were buried in a small cemetery on the slope of the hill. The Neolithic II people used a pottery ('combed ware') with a red slipped surface decorated by drawing a comb-like tool over the surface (pl. Ib); stone was used for tools and domestic vessels. The Neolithic II sites so far investigated seem to have been abandoned by about 3000 BC.

It is possible that even before this date a further group of newcomers came to the island. The material civilisation of the new settlers is termed 'Chalcolithic' (from the Greek word for copper) because of their use, however limited, of copper tools. The Chalcolithic site of Erimi in south Cyprus, close to Episkopi, is well-known; the houses were round and the walls built partly of stone, partly of mud-brick; a copper chisel was found. The dead were buried in small pit-graves inside the huts. The pottery was carefully painted, the vessels being decorated with a wide range of linear patterns in a dark paint on a light background. Another type of pottery had a red slipped surface. Small and very stylised human figures with outstretched arms, carved in soft stone are typical of this period, especially in south west Cyprus. Only the upper part of one of these figures and fragments of pottery are represented in the collection.

The large number of coastal and inland sites found distributed throughout the island suggests that these people were more successful settlers than their predecessors; indeed, in some areas,

Plate II: Fragments of vases, one spouted, of Red-on-White ware. Neolithic. From *Vrysi*, Ayios Epiktitos. Ht. of largest sherd 0·138 [1972.919–922].

such as the Akamas peninsula in the far west, population seems to have been greater than at any subsequent time. The Chalcolithic I period lasted until somewhere about 2500 BC, when many of the sites were deserted. Some such natural catastrophe as a plague or prolonged drought may have been responsible.

There is a period after this disaster when archaeological evidence is at the moment extremely scanty; the site of Ambelikou near Soloi, on the west coast, possibly helps to fill the transition between the Chalcolithic I period and the Early Bronze Age.

# II. The Bronze Age

## THE EARLY, MIDDLE AND LATE CYPRIOT PERIODS

It is not certain how metal technology first reached Cyprus, though it may have been introduced by new arrivals from overseas who came from Anatolia as refugees from the disturbances which mark the end of the Early Bronze Age II period in that area (*c.* 2300 BC). Certainly these were men versed in metal working, who were probably attracted by the rich deposits of copper-bearing rocks in the Troodos foothills. They settled first in the river valleys from Nicosia westwards to the sea, also near the sea at the west end of the Kyrenia mountains, and possibly in a small area of south Cyprus. Besides their tools and weapons, the Early Cypriot settlers brought with them new burial customs and new types of pottery.

No occupation site has yet been investigated, but a number of tombs, made either in natural clefts or in chambers cut out of the rock, have been excavated, and many objects, particularly pottery, left as gifts for the dead, have been found. Most of the pottery is Red Polished ware. Much of it is undecorated, but some of the vessels have simple linear patterns incised on them. A typical vessel-shape is the jug with flat base, high neck and cutaway spout. Red Polished ware was to have a long history and the final traces of its influence did not disappear until *c.* 1500 BC.

The three phases into which the Early Cypriot period is divided correspond largely to changes and development in pottery. The best known Early Cypriot I site is in the *Vounous* cemetery, near Bellapais, in the foothills behind the fertile coastal plain of Kyrenia. But the Early Bronze Age period is still somewhat confused and it is most likely that Early Cypriot I, in spite of the terminology, is not the earliest stage. The so-called Philia culture, which takes its name from one of a group of sites in the western half of the central plain in the Ovgos valley, has produced copper objects, and pottery which are very probably antecedent to the earliest material found at *Vounous*; Early Cypriot I should therefore be regarded as secondary to the Philia stage culture.

Plate III: Black-topped Red Polished bottle and conical cup. Early Cypriot. From tomb 92, *Vounous*, Bellapais. Ht. 0·262 [1940.163]; Ht. 0·15 [1940.166].

ANCIENT CYPRUS

EARLY CYPRIOT I-II

Red Polished ware (1-7)
Fig. Ia

# THE BRONZE AGE

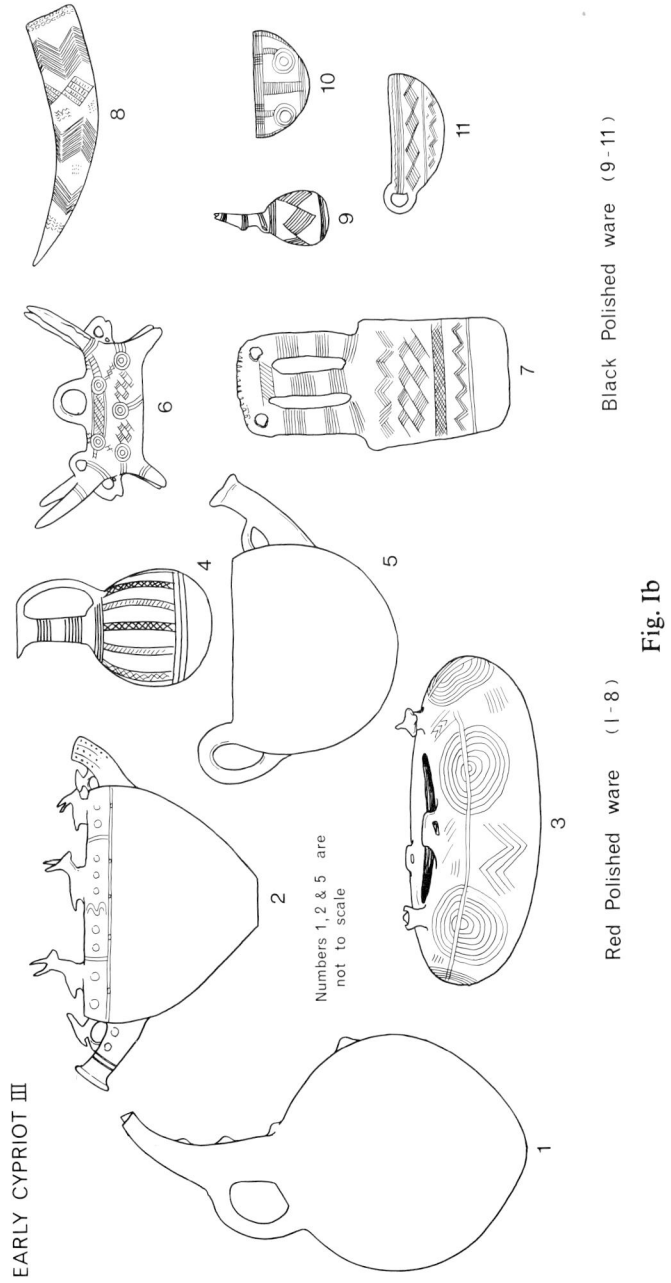

EARLY CYPRIOT III

Numbers 1, 2 & 5 are not to scale

Red Polished ware (1-8)   Black Polished ware (9-11)

Fig. Ib

Excavations at *Vounous* have recovered a series of tomb groups belonging not only to Early Cypriot I but also to the whole of the Early Cypriot and Middle Cypriot periods. It is noteworthy that during this long period the shapes of the storage vessels—jugs, jars and amphorae—change so that gradually the flat bases that distinguished Early Cypriot I are replaced by the completely round-bodied vessels of Early Cypriot III. This must reflect a change not only in taste but in the amenities in the homes of those for whom these pots were made—flat-based pots belong where there are shelves and well-made tables, and level, paved floors; round bases suggest a rougher home, where pot-hollows can be scraped in earth floors. This change in shape is illustrated by the bottle from *Vounous* Tomb 92 (pl. III), on the one hand, and the double-necked gourd-jug (pl. V) of Early Cypriot III on the other (see also figs. Ia, Ib). By Early Cypriot III the use of incised ornament had become more common, and the pattern-work more intricate. A filling of gypsum paste in the incisions helped the designs to stand out from the ground-colour of the pots. By controlling the firing of their wares, the potters producing Red Polished ware could also make a two-colour fabric—red and black—so that many vessels (e.g. pl. III) have black tops and red bodies. Many small bowls have a red body, black lip and black interior. A completely black fabric (Black Polished ware) was popular in Early Cypriot III; the vessels are nearly always small and invariably have incised patterns (see fig. Ib, 9–11). The potters were also gifted modellers, as can be seen both in the figures of animals, birds and snakes added in the round or in relief to normal types of vessel (e.g. the stags on the large basin, and the bulls on the pyxis, fig. Ib, 2–3) and in the vessels made in the shapes, sometimes rather stylised, of animals, like the stag-vase (pl. VI) and the double bull-vase (fig. Ib, 6), even more stylised are the 'plank-shaped' human figures (fig. Ib, 7), many of which were found in the Early Cypriot III tombs at Lapithos.

The wide distribution of Early Cypriot III sites suggests steady expansion throughout the period. Our understanding of the process would be greater were more known of the occupation sites through excavation. A partly dug site at Alambra, in central Cyprus, revealed a two-room house with courtyard and pens for domestic animals. Some insight into the daily activities of these Early Cypriots can be gained from a series of clay models found in tombs

# THE BRONZE AGE

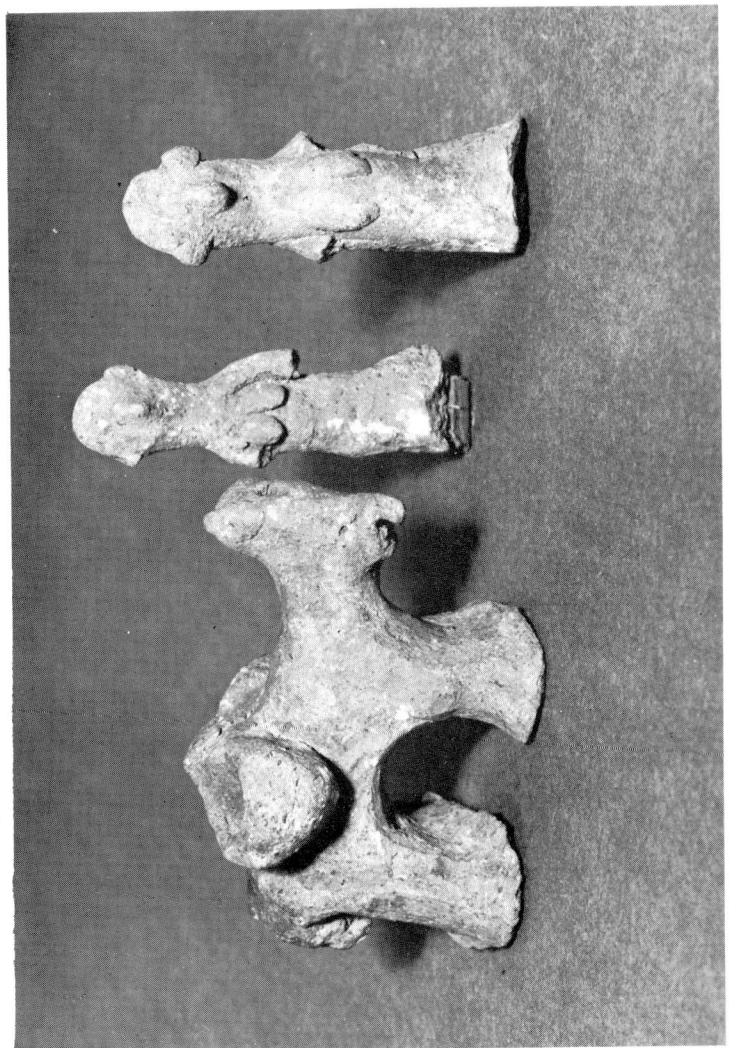

Plate IV: Pack donkey with panniers and two women broken from vessels. Early Cypriot III. L. 0.09 [1888.623]; Ht. 0.08 [1888.643].

Plate V: Red Polished III double-spouted gourd-shaped jug. Early Cypriot III. Given by Mrs. Guy Dickens. Ht. 0·245 [1916.53].

Plate VI: Red Polished vase in the shape of a stylised stag. Early Cypriot III. Ht. 0·17 [1888.624].

at *Vounous* and elsewhere. Some of the more elaborate *genre* models show men ploughing with ox-teams, worshippers with their offerings at open air shrines, and even a complete sacred enclosure in which we see penned animals ready to be offered to the gods whose images are modelled on the wall, and a whole array of seated and standing officiants and worshippers; there is even an outsider shown peering over the top of the wall at what is taking place within the sanctuary. Some of these *genre* scenes either in relief or the round, decorate large basins or great jugs; there are representations of women grinding corn, making bread and pouring liquids, of men tending animals and tilling the land. The little pack donkey of pl. IV is broken from the vase it once decorated, as are the two roughly made figures of women illustrated on the same plate.

Before the end of the Early Cypriot period there is clear evidence for occasional trade between Cyprus and the Syro-Palestinian area, Egypt and Crete. This evidence is of chronological importance, for the find of an Early Minoan III painted pot in an Early Cypriot III tomb at Lapithos, and a Middle Minoan I (Kamares ware) cup in a Middle Cypriot I tomb at Karmi suggest that the end of Early Cypriot III must be close to 2000 BC.

The Early Bronze Age passes imperceptibly into the Middle Bronze Age in Cyprus, so that the main distinction between Early Cypriot III and Middle Cypriot I is the appearance of pottery with painted ornaments ('White Painted' ware), though its emergence had been foreshadowed already in Early Cypriot III. Burial customs continued unchanged. Red Polished ware continued throughout the Middle Cypriot period, though its quality became increasingly inferior both in form and fabric (fig. IIa, 10–11). Vases of White Painted ware were decorated with red brown or dark brown paint laid on a light ground; though originally the paint was burnished and had a glossy finish, much of the later work was executed in matt paint. The designs are almost invariably linear; shapes (which overlap to some extent with Red Polished ware) grow fussier with the passing of time—the clear line and firm patternwork of the Middle Cypriot I jug (pl. VII), was replaced in Middle Cypriot III by a degree of over-elaboration that is almost baroque. The love of modelling in the round and in relief that is so characteristic of the Early Cypriot period largely vanished in Middle Cypriot times.

Our knowledge of the Middle Cypriot period depends very

# THE BRONZE AGE

Plate VII: White Painted jug, the decoration in lustrous red paint. Middle Cypriot. Given by Sir Philip Antrobus. Ht. 0·248 [1963.1638].

largely on the evidence of cemeteries. Only at Kalopsidha, in the east half of the central plain, has an occupation site been investigated in any detail, though traces of Middle Cypriot III occupation have been studied in the lowest levels of a number of Late Cypriot settlements (e.g. Enkomi and Myrtou, *Pigadhes*). At Kalopsidha a house of ten rooms, including storerooms, workshops and a courtyard was uncovered, revealing a very much more sophisticated complex than the simple two-room house from the Early Cypriot III site at Alambra, mentioned above.

The Middle Cypriot period does not seem to have been peaceful, to judge both from the profusion of weapons recovered from cemetery sites, and from the fortification of a number of occupation sites. Many of these fortified sites are too far from the coast to suppose that they were built for protection from sea-borne enemies, and it seems probable that the island was disunited for much of the Middle Cypriot period. One important fort which may have been first built in the Middle Cypriot period is, in fact, near the coast, at *Nitovikla*, on the south side of the Karpas peninsula.

In the Middle Cypriot period there is increasing evidence for the island's contacts with her overseas neighbours. During Middle Cypriot III in particular, Cypriot goods (especially pottery) travelled to the Syro-Palestinian area, while many items made in that region, and in Anatolia, have been found in Cyprus. The copper of Cyprus must have been an important element in this trade, which seems to have encouraged the founding of many sites on or near the coast, particularly in the south-east. Many of the wealthy towns of the succeeding Late Cypriot period owed their foundation to this movement, which illustrates the end of the island's isolation from the world of her neighbours, and the first of the steps by which she was increasingly to lose that 'Kyprios character', to which Aeschylus long after referred. There are hints of regionalism at this time, seen most clearly in the preference in eastern Cyprus for the pottery fabric called Red-on-Black ware (pl. VIII). The surface of these vessels is covered in a black wash, with simple linear patterns added in red paint, by the use of a multiple brush. Certain metal types, including dress pins, more characteristic of eastern Cyprus than elsewhere (pl. IX) reinforce this suggestion.

The beginnings of the Late Cypriot period belong to the sixteenth century BC; the period, divisible into three main and several sub-

Plate VIII: Red-on-Black tankard-shaped jug, typical of East Cyprus. Middle Cypriot. Ht. 0·195 [1953.220].

phases, lasted for some five centuries, and saw Cyprus drawn further and further into international trade and hence international politics. By its close, foreign influences on the island had been strong enough to extinguish almost completely its own distinctive cultural traits; this process was to be repeated more than once in Cyprus' later history. Yet the Late Cypriot period began without

Plate IX. Middle Cypriot Bronzes: a. Mushroom-headed toggle pin (tip missing). From Eylenja, *Leondari Vouno*, given by the Cyprus Exploration Fund. L. 0·108 [1888.1318]. b. Pin, given by G. J. Chester. L. 0·09 [1883.160]. c. Rat-tanged dirk, the upper part of the midrib decorated with herringbone pattern. L. 0·303 [1918.28]. d. Pair of tweezers. Given by Sir Arthur Evans. L. 0·12 [1927.1395].

any apparent change of population or dramatic change in a material culture in which Early Cypriot antecedents are still to be seen. Late Cypriot I seems to have been an uneasy period, in which the fortresses remained in use, some of them suffering destruction; graves containing mass burials found both in east and west Cyprus may imply the ravages of war, though a lethal epidemic may have been equally responsible. Perhaps because the times were unsettled, there was little development or innovation in material civilisation in Late Cypriot I. The metal industry made few technical advances,

# THE BRONZE AGE

a

b

Plate X: a. White Slip II crater (mixing vessel). Late Cypriot II. From the Cesnola Collection. Ht. 0·234 [1911.333]. b. Base Ring I bowl with wavy band in relief. Late Cypriot I. Given by Sir Leonard Woolley, from the Sandwith Collection. D. 0·161 [C. 86].

although evidently abundant copper was available to the smiths; weapons, tools and personal ornaments were of plain design and simple technique (pl. IX). Much pottery continued to be made in the old hand-made traditions of Early and Middle Cypriot times, even though potters in neighbouring countries were almost all using the wheel; wheel-made pottery was imported in appreciable quantities. But the beginning of the Late Cypriot period is marked by the appearance of two important new pottery fabrics, which between them supplied most of the fine table-ware through much of the Late Bronze Age. The first is known by the name 'Base Ring' ware (fig. IIb, 4–7) given to it by Sir John Myres from the very characteristic ring bases that are a feature of nearly every vessel in this fabric. It is a hand-made fabric, produced with great care, the vessels having extremely thin walls, fired at high temperature, usually covered by a thin but highly polished dark brown slip, often decorated in relief (pls. Xb, XIb). The commonest shapes are bowls with wishbone handles, jugs with tall necks and flaring mouths (pl. XIb) and juglets whose shape has been thought to resemble a poppy seed head, implying perhaps that these vessels had been designed to hold opium dissolved in liquid. Many of these Base Ring ware juglets were exported from Cyprus to the Levant (examples in the Near Eastern gallery) and Egypt (examples in the Dynastic gallery); their presence in Egyptian contexts, in particular, provides important synchronisms between the chronology of the Late Cypriot period and the XVIII Dynasty in Egypt. The second fabric, 'White Slip' ware, is also of some technical excellence. Its name comes from the thick white slip used by the potters to cover their rather coarse fabric; this slip was lightly polished, and may be lustrous. Decoration is invariably linear, in orange, brown or black paint; in some of the finest examples a two-colour scheme was employed, but this technique was not common. The most popular shape was a round-based bowl with a wishbone handle (the so-called 'milk-bowl') (fig. IIb, 3) but jugs and juglets (fig. IIb, 1–2) craters (pl. Xa) and tankards (pl. XIa) were more occasionally made. As the years passed, the quality of both Base Ring ware and White Slip ware deteriorated, though they continued to be made in enormous quantities until the end of Late Cypriot II, *c.* 1200 BC, or later.

Some Cypriots, at least, could read and write from a date early in the Late Cypriot period; regular and close contacts with their more

THE BRONZE AGE

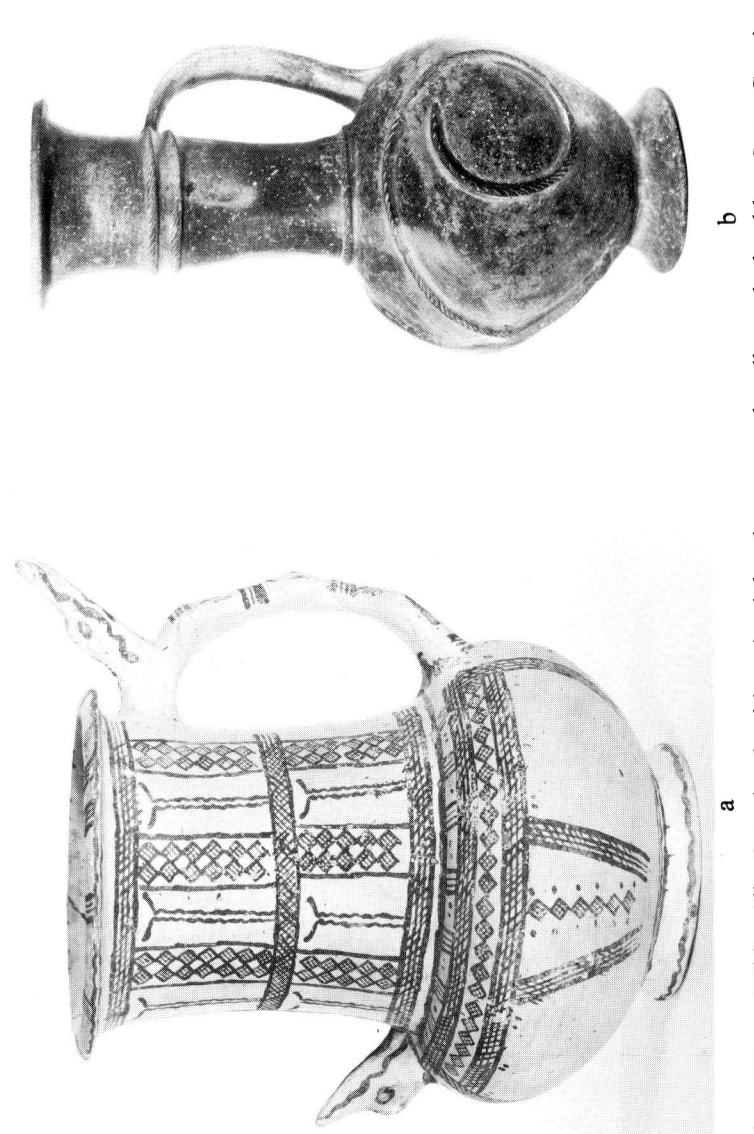

Plate XI: a. White Slip I tankard with animal head spur on handle and shoulder. Late Cypriot I. From Magounda, Paphos. Ht. 0·23 [1968.1154]. b. Base Ring I jug with incised relief decoration. Late Cypriot II. Ht. 0·331 [1968.85].

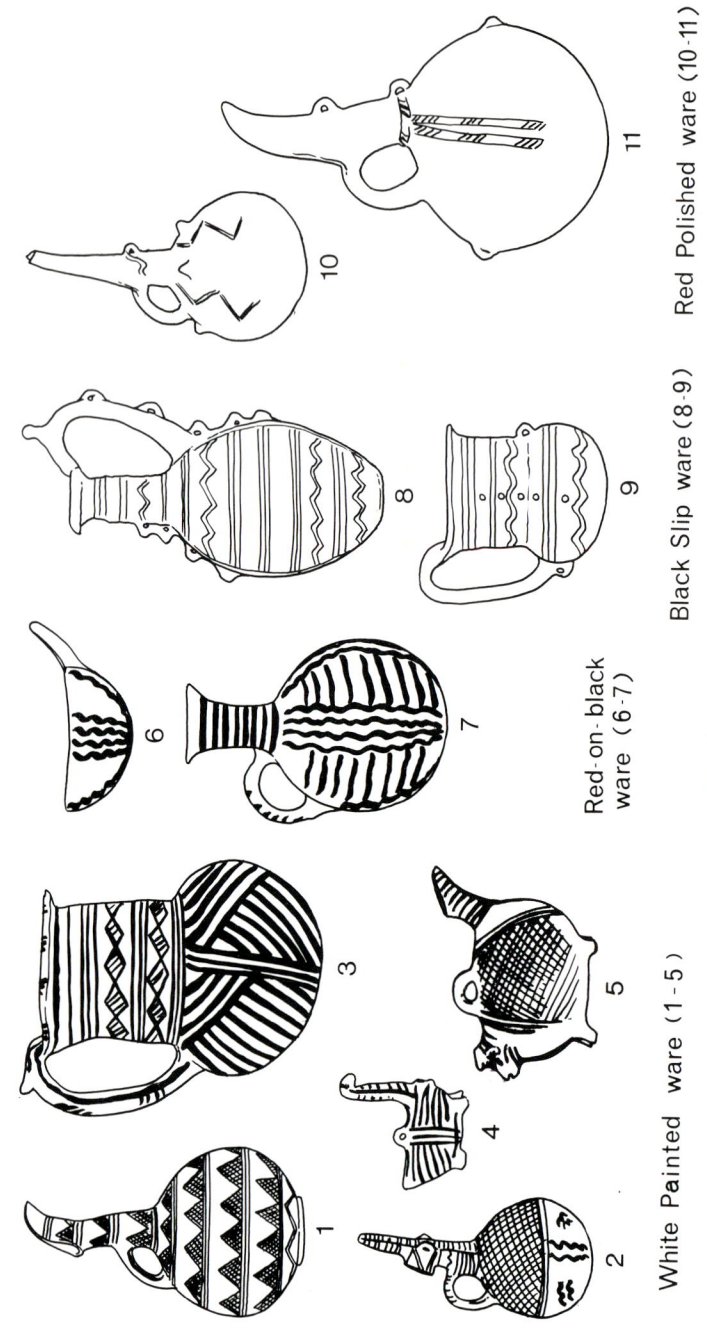

Fig. IIa

THE BRONZE AGE

LATE CYPRIOT

White Slip ware (1-3)

Base Ring ware (4-7)

Mycenaean (8-13) and other imported pottery (14)

Fig. IIb

29

advanced continental neighbours would have taught them the advantages of writing. It is not yet known by exactly what means they developed their own system of closely related scripts still known to scholars as 'Cypro-Minoan' from resemblances to the syllabic scripts of Minoan Crete. This script has been found in the form of continuous texts on baked clay tablets (the earliest of *c.* 1500 BC, from Enkomi), as well as very brief inscriptions incised or painted on pottery vessels, impressed on metal objects and included in the design of seal stones. No satisfactory decipherment has yet been proposed, but intensive study continues, handicapped chiefly by the scarcity of texts of any length. Even if the script itself shows affinities with that of the contemporary Aegean, the cushion-shaped tablets, and the fact that they are kiln-baked imply the influence of the Near East. Although the tablets known so far have been discovered at Enkomi, bone styli of the type that must have been used for writing have been found at Kouklia (Palaeopaphos) and Hala Sultan Tekke (near Larnaka), and it seems probable that literacy, though very limited, was general, at least in the major towns. Use of the script persisted, at Enkomi at least, until the very end of the Late Cypriot period; it is difficult to believe there is no direct link with the Cypriot syllabic script of the Archaic and Classical period (below, p. 42) used for writing Greek, but this has yet to be demonstrated satisfactorily.

At much the same time, Cypriots discovered the advantages of using seals, no doubt from the same sources as they learned the value of writing. Seals had for long been in use in the Near East to identify ownership of property, to endorse contracts and to authorise actions in societies where only a very small group of highly privileged administrators could read and write. A number of Near Eastern cylinder seals were brought to Cyprus from early in the Late Cypriot period, and a school of Cypriot seal-cutters appeared whose work reflects, sometimes rather crudely, the styles of the cylinder seals of Syria and elsewhere (for the developed impression of one of these seals, see pl. XIIa). Before long, seal styles were also to show Aegean influences, sometimes, as in the case of some stamp seals of Late Cypriot III (twelfth century BC), very strongly.

The use of seals and the development of writing are but two of many indications that show Cyprus' increasing participation in the

a (Enlarged)

b

Plate XII: a. Impression of a cylinder seal. Late Cypriot. From Pyla, M. Ohnefalsch-Richter Collection. Ht. of cylinder 0·028 [1896.5]. b. Gold funerary frontlet, decorated with embossed spirals, circles and flowers. Late Cypriot II. Perhaps from Enkomi. L. 0·223 [1962.244].

sophisticated commercial and political life of the East Mediterranean in the period of the New Kingdom in Egypt (*c.* 1558–1075 BC). From the middle of the fifteenth century BC, Cyprus became of increasing importance to Mycenaean Greece, so that, in place of the tiny trickle of goods that had reached Cyprus from the West in the previous centuries, imported Mycenaean pottery in enormous quantities appeared in the island throughout the fourteenth and much of the thirteenth centuries BC (fig. IIb, 8–13). Such pottery has been found at sites throughout the island, both in settlements, and in tombs. It is particularly abundant at the rich sites of the east (Enkomi), south east (Pyla, Larnaka, Hala Sultan Tekke) and south coasts (Maroni, Episkopi and Kouklia) which may reasonably be regarded as the chief ports that handled overseas trade. Yet the sheer mass of Mycenaean pottery is so great that some scholars suppose that Mycenaean colonies were set up in Cyprus during the fourteenth century BC and that this pottery was locally made. Against this view must be set the fact that there is virtually no other indication of the presence of Mycenaeans in the fourteenth and thirteenth centuries. The more probable explanation seems to be that Cyprus was of immense economic importance to the Mycenaeans, who both sought the raw copper obtainable in its manufacturing towns and valued the island as an entrepôt for their other commercial activities in the Near East. Very regular trading voyages were made between Mycenaean ports (especially those of the Peloponnese) and Cyprus, and part, at least, of this trade was concerned with the supply to Cyprus of fine table-wares made in Mycenaean factories—especially the large craters (mixing bowls) decorated in the 'pictorial style' (see fragments on display and fig. IIb, 9) on which were painted processions of chariots, and bulls and birds. Cypriots evidently treasured such vases and often chose to be buried with them.

The trade of which we are speaking meant an increase of real wealth in Cyprus. The wealth of the dead was no longer expressed only in terms of the locally made goods that were laid in their graves, but in objects of gold and silver, in *bijouterie* from Egypt and the Levant, in luxury objects, of such exotic materials as Egyptian calcite, Near Eastern or African ivory, and Levantine faience. Cypriots worked in these new materials, as witness the (rather crude) gold frontlet (pl. XIIb) used to cover the eyes of the dead, probably found at Enkomi; the material may well be Egyptian, the style of ornament learned from the Mycenaeans, but the workmanship is unmistakably Cypriot.

Cyprus in Late Cypriot II (fourteenth and thirteenth centuries BC) developed upon a scale that has seldom been repeated. The settlement and cemetery sites already identified throughout the island suggest a very substantial population, with a sharp contrast between urban communities with a strong industrial element in their economy (copper-working, in particular) and rural settlements where a more traditional way of life continued. But even here there was change, for many areas of virtually virgin land (many square miles in the Kormakiti peninsula, for example) were occupied and brought into cultivation for the first time. Such a development is entirely consistent with the great expansion of urban populations elsewhere. Between the rural settlements and the manufacturing and port towns of the coastal areas are a number of inland sites—Nicosia for example, and Ayios Sozomenos—whose obvious prosperity seems likely to have come from their control of the inland communications by which the products of the copper mines were brought down to the manufacturing centres.

If Cyprus was indeed of such economic importance and so prosperous, the object of attention from both her European and Asiatic neighbours, should there not be reference to her in contemporary texts? In fact, a majority of scholars believe that Cyprus must be identified with the *Alashiya* to which there are many references in documents from Egypt, Syria and Anatolia. These documents show that *Alashiya* sent copper to Egypt, and received silver, ebony and other merchandise in exchange; she traded with Syria and Anatolia in copper in return for manufactured goods. *Alashiya* was a country with its own king; near the end of the thirteenth century BC it was important enough to have its own fleet. Early in the twelfth century BC it was overrun by the Peoples of the Sea. Cyprus and *Alashiya* may have been one and the same, but the final and convincing proof is still elusive.

These halcyon days lasted for nearly two centuries, until the closing years of the thirteenth century BC, when Cyprus was called upon to share in the tribulations of her more powerful neighbours; the vicissitudes through which she passed brought first a great catastrophe, datable to *c.* 1200 BC (seen particularly clearly in a great destruction at Enkomi and other major centres), then a very remarkable renaissance that can be seen in every aspect of material civilisation. It is very tempting to connect these events with the contemporary upheavals in Mycenaean Greece in which many of the great centres (Mycenae, Sparta, Pylos) suffered destruction, followed by a partial diaspora of the surviving population. Some of the fugitives undoubtedly reached Cyprus *c.* 1200 BC, where they introduced many features of their own material culture of which Cyprus had previously known nothing, even at the height of her trade contact with Greece. Their presence has been most clearly established at Enkomi as a result of the very extensive excavation of that site, but their traces can also be seen at Maa, Kouklia, Pyla, Sinda, Larnaka and Ayios Sozomenos. Their arrival coincided with the development of new and sophisticated architectural schemes and building techniques, particularly the use of ashlar masonry. A revolution took place in the metal industry, involving the introduction of new technical expertise as well as the appearance of a whole new repertory of design and ornament, much of it having its roots in Mycenaean Greece. It was probably at this date that the so-called 'oxhide' ingots were introduced, as an administrative convenience for handling the newly smelted copper both in the home market, and for overseas shipment. The new-found versatility of the bronze-smiths and bronze-founders is particularly clearly seen in their tripod stands (examples are on display), vessels and miniature sculpture, where the advantages of the *cire-perdue* process were exploited to the full. Notice in particular the statuette of a naked woman (pl. XIII) standing on an 'oxhide' ingot, perhaps the female counterpart of the more famous statuette of a spear-brandishing warrior standing on an ingot, now in the Nicosia museum, found at Enkomi. It has been suggested that these two figures may represent male and female deities who between them both protected the metal industry and guaranteed its productivity. It is even possible that the temple authorities in some of the Cypriot manufacturing towns were responsible for the management of the metal industry.

If it is true that Mycenaean refugees played a leading part in the cultural renaissance of Cyprus in the twelfth century BC, it must be recognised that their own character had been somewhat altered by their change of home. Apart from the influence of Cyprus itself, they were affected by other refugees from Syria and Palestine who, in their turn, had much to contribute. The twelfth century BC in Cyprus saw the brief flowering of a material civilisation conspicuous for the excellence not only of its architecture, bronze-working, and ceramic production but also of its jewellery, ivory-carving and seal-cutting, an excellence for which Cypriots,

Plate XIII: Bronze statuette of a naked woman, perhaps the goddess 'Astarte', standing on an 'oxhide' ingot. Late Cypriot III. From the Bomford Collection. Ht. 0·099 [1971.888].

Levantines and the peoples of the Aegean were collectively responsible. It is clear from the continued appearance in Cyprus of successive styles of Mycenaean pottery that other groups of refugees from Greece and, probably, from Crete too, found their way to Cyprus during the course of the twelfth century BC. Conditions in the island seem to have deteriorated steadily as the century advanced, so that the population dwindled almost to the point of extinction in all but a few of the old urban centres, such as Kouklia, Episkopi, Larnaka, Lapithos and, perhaps, Dhali. The transition between the end of the Late Bronze Age (Late Cypriot) and the start of the early Iron Age (Cypro-Geometric) is an almost imperceptible process, dated *c.* 1050 BC, the best index of which is a relatively slight change in the style of painted pottery (the replacement of Proto-White Painted ware by White Painted I ware). Iron had been known and used for over a century already; the change was marked by no violent catastrophe—before it happened, but not long before, the Greek language took firm root, not, indeed, as the sole language, but perhaps already the most important. The first, and most vital step in the Hellenisation of Cyprus had been taken.

# III. The Iron Age

## THE CYPRO-GEOMETRIC ARCHAIC AND CLASSIC PERIODS

### THE CYPRO-GEOMETRIC PERIOD

The end of the Bronze Age, *c.* 1050 BC, had coincided with the disappearance of nearly all the old-established settlements in Cyprus, and a consequent great reduction in the island's population, and in the virtual extinction of overseas contacts. Not since the end of the Chalcolithic period had there been so severe a reverse in the island's affairs. For the next three centuries—the Early Iron Age—we know much less of what went on in Cyprus than we do for the Late Bronze Age. This is the 'Dark Age', and its obscurity may be compared with a similar phenomenon in most neighbouring regions at this period, not least in Greece. What little we do know comes very largely from the excavation of cemeteries. There is a great need for excavation at a number of settlement sites occupied from the later eleventh century BC onwards; unfortunately, suitable sites have been difficult to identify.

The period from *c.* 1050 to 700 BC is called the 'Cypro-Geometric' period, further subdivided into Cypro-Geometric I, II and III. The name is taken from the characteristic linear-ornament used for pottery decoration—triangles, zig-zags, hatched lozenges; it is not to be confused with the term 'Geometric' which is applied to approximately the same period in Greece. It is indeed a paradox of Cypriot history that the island's links with Greece should have grown so slender so soon after the arrival of the last contingent of refugee immigrants from Greece. As we have just seen everything points to the fact that it was these immigrants who introduced the Greek tongue to Cyprus, where over the coming generations it established itself as the dominant (but not the only) language.

Although nearly all the settlements, large and small, of the Late Bronze Age had been abandoned before the middle of the eleventh century BC, many of the known Cypro-Geometric I sites are in the vicinity of important Bronze Age predecessors. Salamis was established close to Enkomi; at Curium, Palaeopaphos and Lapithos, Cypro-Geometric I cemeteries have been found near Late Bronze Age sites. On the other hand, the Cypro-Geometric I settlement at Kition was built directly on Late Bronze Age ruins. At Amathus and probably at Polis-tis-Khrysokhou, completely new sites were chosen. Each of these was later to develop into one of the island's city-kingdoms.

In the cemeteries of Curium and Lapithos, at least, the design of some rock-cut Cypro-Geometric I tombs, with squarish chambers and long entrance passages narrower at the top than the bottom, closely recalls a standard Mycenaean type, and symbolises the strength of the Mycenaean inheritance with which the period starts. And though much had changed, burial customs themselves continued previous Cypriot tradition, where the chamber-tomb served as a family sepulchre, one tomb sometimes continuing in use over many generations. Offerings of pottery vessels, sometimes filled with food or drink, continued to be buried with the dead, sometimes in great numbers; other gifts were offered more sparingly. These included weapons of iron, bronze vessels and, in a few cases, personal ornaments of gold.

Cypro-Geometric I pottery, both in shape and decoration, shows continuity with the Mycenaean past. There is much that recalls Proto-White Painted ware of Late Cypriot IIIB, and influence from sub-Minoan Crete has also been recognised. Nearly all fine pottery was now thrown on the fast wheel. The decorated pottery of the Iron Age in Cyprus has been studied systematically by Swedish scholars, in particular Professor Einar Gjerstad. Seven 'Types' have been distinguished, which between them cover the whole period from the beginning in Cypro-Geometric I (*c.* 1050 BC) until the end of the Classical period, *c.* 325 BC. Within each 'Type' a number of different fabrics are represented, some of which (for example 'White Painted') last throughout the period. Roughly speaking, pottery Types I, II and III coincide with the division of the Cypriot Geometric period into I (1050–950 BC), II (950–850) and III (850–700). But it should be noted that Type I, notionally characteristic of Cypro-Geometric I, continued into Cypro-Geometric II and overlaps Type II; there is a similar relationship between Types II and III. There are hints in this, surely, of the co-existence of

THE IRON AGE

Plate XIV: White Painted I–II barrel-shaped jug. Cypro-Geometric II. Given by P. Hobson from the Goldie Collection. Ht. 0·20 [1961.451].

a

b

Plate XV: a. Bichrome III stemmed cup, decorated with birds. Cypro-Geometric III–Cypro-Archaic I. Ht. 0·105 [1961.413]. b. Bichrome I stemmed cup decorated with panels of geometric ornament. Cypro-Geometric I. From the Flower Collection. Ht. 0·11 [1885.522].

## THE IRON AGE

successive workshop traditions in pottery-making.

The best-known pottery fabric is 'White Painted' ware, distinguished by the use of a matt dark brown to black paint as decoration on the light ground colour of the clay (pl. XIV). Very closely related, though less common, was 'Bichrome' ware, in which a matt red paint was also used to enliven the dark brown of the dominant patternwork (pl. XV–XVI, fig. IIIa. IIIa, 6–7). Care should be taken

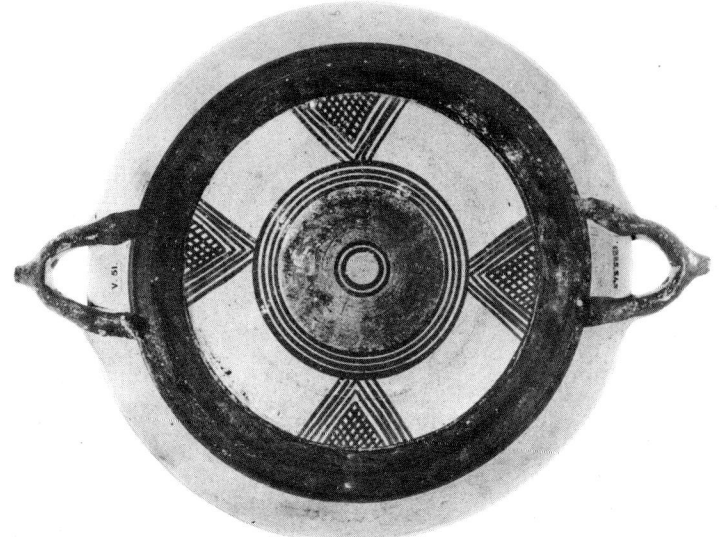

Plate XVI: Bichrome II–III two-handled plate. Cypro-Geometric III. From the Flower Collection. D. 0·23 [1885.545].

not to confuse the 'White Painted' pottery of the Geometric period with the 'White Painted' pottery of the Middle Bronze age (see p. 20). 'Black Slip' (see fig. IIIa, 8–9) and 'Plain White' are less common wares, confined to a limited range of shapes. Rather later than the first appearance of these fabrics is 'Black-on-Red' ware, thought to have been introduced from southern Anatolia or Syria (pl. XXI is a late example; fig. IIIa, 4–5).

Popular vessel shapes, in tomb material at least, include large amphorae (some with handles on the neck, others on the belly), craters, barrel-shaped jugs (pl. XIV), cups and plates (pl. XVI). As the Cypro-Geometric period advanced, the austerity of the linear decoration relaxed, and White Painted III and Bichrome III designs sometimes include birds (pl. XVa, fig. IIIa, 7), animals or, more rarely, human beings. Vases in the shape of animals or birds are occasionally found (fig. IIIa, 6).

It is very doubtful whether Geometric Cyprus was politically unified, though the lines of division can hardly be discerned from archaeological evidence alone. Pottery, and later sculpture, in east Cyprus have certain characteristics that distinguish that region from the western part of the island. But other evidence suggests something much more complex than this. The very existence of the city-kingdoms in the early Archaic period implies separate territorial identities; such a system almost certainly developed in the 'darkness' of the Geometric period. It may even be that kingship as an institution was a Mycenaean legacy. There is a Geometric cemetery near the cities of Salamis, Kition, Paphos, Amathus, Curium, Marion, Soloi, Tamassos, Idalion, Lapithos and Kyrenia—strongly suggesting that their foundation dates lie within the Geometric period. Moreover, the division of language which is to be seen from the Archaic period certainly goes back to an earlier date, and we may suppose that the divisions of race implicit in Arcado-Cypriot Greek, in the undeciphered Eteo-Cypriot, and Phoenician also imply political division.

We saw above (p. 30) that a syllabic script ('Cypro-Minoan') was used by literate Cypriot communities in the Late Bronze Age; it survived until the very end of that period. The script is undeciphered, but the language it expresses is not Greek. Before the end of Cypro-Geometric III (*c.* 700 BC), a similar syllabary\* was again in use in Cyprus. Though proof of continuity is lacking, we may suppose that the later syllabary—the 'Cypriot' syllabary—depends in some way upon Cypro-Minoan. In the seventh century, when the Cypriot syllabary becomes common it was used to express two unrelated languages—Arcado-Cypriot Greek (apparently introduced at the end of the Bronze Age) and Eteo-Cypriot, perhaps the surviving indigeneous language of Cyprus in the Bronze Age.

\* A syllabary is a method of language notation in which each sign represents not a single sound (as in an alphabet) but a syllable—i.e. a consonant–plus–vowel, or on occasions a vowel alone. For example, separate signs will be used to represent the syllables -a-, -ka-, -sa-.

## THE IRON AGE

The Cypriot syllabary has between 50 and 60 symbols, which vary somewhat in different parts of the island, and at different periods. Most texts are short; the majority are funerary, though many royal names and titles, usually abbreviated, appear on coins (pl. XXVc). The Greek alphabet eventually appeared in Cyprus c. 400 BC, but the syllabary was still in use late in the third century BC. Thereafter it seems to have been abandoned.

The decipherment of the Cypriot syllabary was achieved in the 1870s, much assisted by a number of 'bilingual' inscriptions-syllabic and Phoenician inscriptions on the same stone. The main outline of the decipherment was the work of the English Assyriologist, George Smith.

Eteo-Cypriot, though most common at Amathus (traditionally the home of the 'autochthonous' Cypriots) and in its neighbourhood (e.g. pl. XXVII, fourth century BC, from Polemidhia) is not confined to that city, as recent finds at Paphos have shown. The existence of two languages in one city may here be a special case, since Paphos was a shrine of great sanctity, with an international reputation.

The eminence achieved by some cities even before the end of the Geometric period is exemplified by recent discoveries in the necropolis of Salamis: a large cemetery dating from the early eighth century BC. It included a number of monumental tombs with stone-built burial chambers sunk in the relatively soft bedrock; the tomb-entrance was set in a fine monumental facade reached by a broad, sloping entrance passage, in some cases up to 20 metres long. Although every tomb chamber had, unfortunately, been looted, nearly all the passages were undisturbed with their offerings intact. These included the remains of the vehicles used to bring the dead to the tomb, and the skeletons of the teams of horses that drew them. The horses lay with their iron bits still in their mouths, and their rich trappings of bronze still on their bodies. This type of burial was practised for more than a century at Salamis and, on a more modest scale, is attested elsewhere in Cyprus—at Idalion, Paphos and Patriki, for instance. The tomb architecture suggests links with Gordion, the Phrygian city in central Anatolia, while some of the vehicle-fittings and horse-trappings are very similar to Assyrian equipment seen on palace-reliefs at Nimrud and elsewhere; some of the carved ivories which once decorated wooden furniture are of Phoenician style. One of the earliest of these 'royal'

# ANCIENT CYPRUS

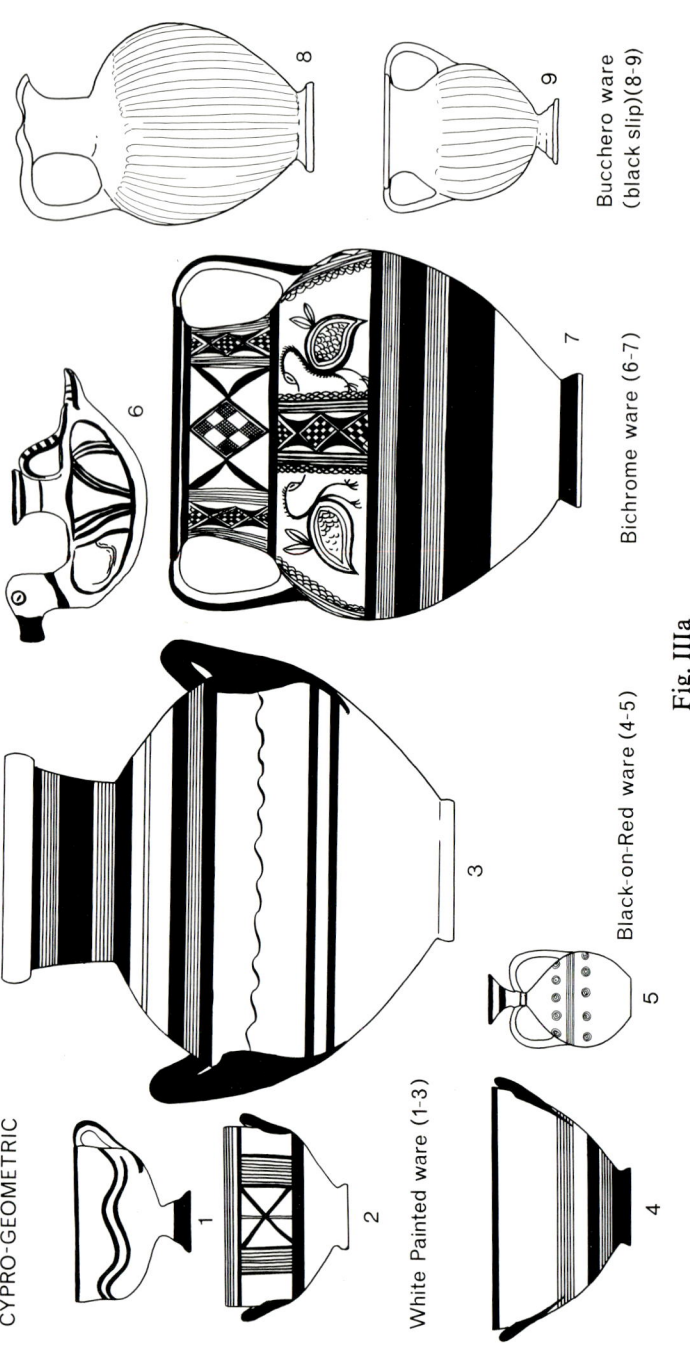

Fig. IIIa

# THE IRON AGE

CYPRO-ARCHAIC

Black-on-Red ware (1-2)   White Painted ware (3-4)   Bichrome ware (5-7)   Phoenician Pottery (8-10)

Fig. IIIb

tombs contained over twenty painted vases made in Athens and the Euboeo-Cycladic area during the second quarter of the eighth century BC. Such diversity of foreign contact marks the end of the 'Dark Age' and a return of the conditions which had brought Cyprus much prosperity in the Late Bronze Age.

This is not the only respect in which recent excavation has changed our understanding of events in Cyprus during Geometric times. At Kition (modern Larnaka), Dr. Karageorghis has uncovered the remains of a very large Phoenician temple first built during the ninth century BC, evidently the work of those Phoenicians who colonised Kition from Tyre. Inscriptions suggest that this building was dedicated to Astarte. The temple was rectangular, $35 \times 22$ metres; its roof was carried on four wooden colonnades, each of seven piers set in square stone bases. The surviving masonry includes a facing course of superbly drafted ashlar blocks, each $3 \cdot 50 \times 1 \cdot 50$ metres. There were four distinct phases in the life of the building, which was only finally abandoned at the end of the fourth century BC, coinciding with the execution, at the orders of Ptolemy, of Pumiathon, last king of Kition, in 312 BC.

It was at one time thought that the Phoenicians had exercised an all-pervasive influence on Cyprus from early in the Bronze Age onwards. Later, ideas changed, and they came to be regarded as 'mere carriers of other people's goods'. The Kition evidence shows that the truth lies somewhere between the two extremes. Despite the completely Phoenician character of the Kition temple, and of many minor antiquities (cf. pottery from the Turabi Tekke cemetery on display, see also fig. IIIb, 8–10), syllabic inscriptions recently found show that both Arcado-Cypriot and Eteo-Cypriot were spoken as well as the Phoenician language in which the ruling Phoenician dynasts inscribed their coins (pl. XXVb).

By the end of the eighth century BC Cyprus had, nominally, become subject to Assyria; this status probably encouraged the spread of Phoenician influence, particularly in the south and east parts of the island, the area of many of the best harbours. A monumental stele of Sargon II, King of Assyria (721–705 BC), said to have been found at Larnaka (now in the Staatliche Museen, East Berlin) records the submission of the Cypriot kings. Further confirmation of the subject status of the island (which the Assyrians knew as *Yatnana*) occurs in documents of the reign of Sennacherib (704–681 BC) and again on the prism of Esarhaddon (680–669 BC) in the British Museum, commemorating the rebuilding of a Palace at Nineveh.

## THE CYPRO-ARCHAIC PERIOD

The ascendancy of Assyria began just before the conventional date, *c.* 700 BC, for the start of the Cypro-Archaic period. This stage (divided into two phases, Cypro-Archaic I and Cypro-Archaic II) covers the seventh and sixth centuries BC, and was one of the most prosperous and vigorous in the island's history. Though it was to be a period when the influence of the Orient was strong in Cyprus,

Plate XVII: Bichrome III cup decorated with fishes. Cypro-Archaic I. D. 0·13 [1969.211].

mainland Greece and Ionia also had a vital part to play. In material culture there was no marked break with the past, though the differences between the east and west halves of the island in painted pottery and sculptural styles can be seen more clearly. White Painted IV and Bichrome IV wares appeared; Type III fabrics for some time continued in production side by side (see above, p. 38). The popularity of Black-on-Red grew, particularly for small vessels (fig. IIIb, 1–2). The occasional attempts at figure-drawing made by the Cypro-Geometric III potters were greatly expanded so that a school of vase-painters who specialised in representational designs arose. Their work is called 'Free-Field' from their liking for a single bold design placed in isolation on the otherwise reserved surface of the vase. Much of their work was Bichrome ('Bichrome IV').

Plate XVIII: Bichrome III jug with a strainer spout, decorated with concentric circles and a bird. Cypro-Archaic I. From the Spencer-Churchill Collection. Ht. 0·232 [1965.138].

# THE IRON AGE

Plate XIX: Bichrome IV jug, decorated in 'Free-Field' style, a bird and lotus blossom. Cypro-Archaic I. From the Cesnola Collection. Ht. 0·185 [1967.1088].

Plate XX: Bichrome IV jug, decorated in 'Free-Field' style, a gazelle and stylised tree. Cypro-Archaic I. Ht. 0·250 [1967.839].

Plate XXI: Black-on-Red ware flask, decorated with a bird facing frontal and concentric circles. Cypro-Archaic II. Perhaps from Dhali, Cesnola Collection. Ht. 0·185 [1933.1678].

Though birds (pls. XVIII, XIX, fig. IIIb, 7), were their most popular themes ('Cypriot bird-jugs'), there was much more besides —bulls, gazelles (pl. XX), horses, warriors or huntsmen on foot or mounted in their chariots, fights, and ships. The cup (pl. XVII) decorated with a zone of fish imitates an East Greek shape, but its fish are local. The Black-on-Red flask (pl. XXI) with perching bird is a very unusual example of the influence of the Free-Field painters on a completely different school of potters.

Evidence of religious activity in Cyprus occurs from the Early Cypriot period onwards, but it is most abundant in Archaic times. Many sanctuaries have been found, quantities of votive offerings have been recovered. Many of these shrines lay outside the settlements to which they belonged, and have a distinctly rustic atmosphere. There are very few temples in the normal sense; worship was an out-door affair, though the holy place (the *temenos*) was enclosed by a wall. The gods were honoured by a variety of offerings at or near the altar; worshippers frequently left behind small painted statuettes of stone or terracotta, either representing themselves as suppliants, or the deity in whose honour they had visited the shrine. Occasionally, these votive figures were life-size or larger. More rarely, bronze statuettes, jewellery, sealstones and scarabs were dedicated. In some cases, dedications were recorded by brief inscriptions in the Cypriot syllabary.

Thousands of votive offerings were found in some sanctuaries. The best known is at Ayia Irini and was excavated by the Swedish Cyprus Expedition. More than 2,000 objects, chiefly terracotta statues and statuettes, dating from the end of the Late Bronze Age until Cypro-Archaic II, were found *in situ*. Notice, in the Myres Room, a group of statuettes from *Kamelarga* at Larnaka, a very small fraction of a votive deposit found by Myres in one of the Archaic sanctuaries of Kition. Similar statuettes (e.g. the horsemen, pl. XXII) were used as tomb-gifts.

Minor sculpture in terracotta had already been developed in the Geometric period but became more popular and more diverse in Archaic times. The Bichrome technique of decoration was common on the myriad figures of worshippers, horsemen (pl. XXII) and animals. There was much variety in technique, including completely hand-made figures (pl. XXIIb), figures whose bodies were wheel-made, heads and limbs hand-made, others with mould-made heads

# THE IRON AGE

(pl. XXIIa) on wheel- or hand-made bodies, or figures that were completely mould-made. Not all the life-size figures were painted (but notice the large bearded head from Salamis, on display). Use of moulds brought greater realism; notice the head of a boy (pl. XXIVb) with short cropped curly hair and feathered eyebrows. Archaic terracottas are an important guide to contemporary costume and ornament, especially in the case of female figures; the woman's head (pl. XXIVa) is decked with an elaborate necklace, pendant and earrings.

Plate XXII: Terracotta statuettes of horsemen. Cypro-Archaic. From Amathus, given by the Trustees of the British Museum. a. Ht. 0·149 [C.261]; b. Ht. 0·121 [C.262].

The first sculptors in stone, whose work appears c. 600 BC, used the soft local limestone; the marble of the Kyrenia mountains was not carved before Ptolemaic times. The ease with which this limestone can be cut produced a mass of very bad work, much of it reminiscent of the poorer kind of peasant wood carvings, and, even in work of higher quality, a blandness that is missing when sculptors have to struggle with a material that makes greater demands upon them. Archaic Cypriot sculpture reflects the influence of neighbouring countries whose successive political ascendancies left their mark upon the island. After the collapse of

Assyria in 612 BC, Cyprus became involved with Egypt. The Pharoah Apries (*c.* 588–568 BC) first defeated the combined forces of Cyprus and Phoenicia on land and sea; it was left to his successor Amasis (568–525 BC) to reduce the Cypriot cities to submission. The Egyptianising period that followed these events in Cyprus is to be seen most closely in sculpture found in mid-sixth century sanctuaries in the south and east; the effect may be seen, in miniature, in the bronze statuette (pl. XXIII) of a young man

Plate XXII: Bronze statuette of a youth wearing an Egyptianising wig and kilt (the legs are missing). Cypro-Archaic II. Ht. 0·063 [1968.89].

wearing the characteristic Egyptian kilt and wig. But Egyptian domination was short-lived, for in 545 BC the kings of Cyprus voluntarily submitted to Cyrus of Persia on terms that ensured their survival in semi-independence. Although the island was included within the Fifth Satrapy, the city kings were sufficiently free to issue their own coinages. This new political status stimulated contact between Cyprus and the Greek world, in particular with East Greece. The evidence of this is to be seen, for instance, in limestone sculpture such as the large bearded head (cover). Fine table pottery made in several Greek centres, particularly Athens, and

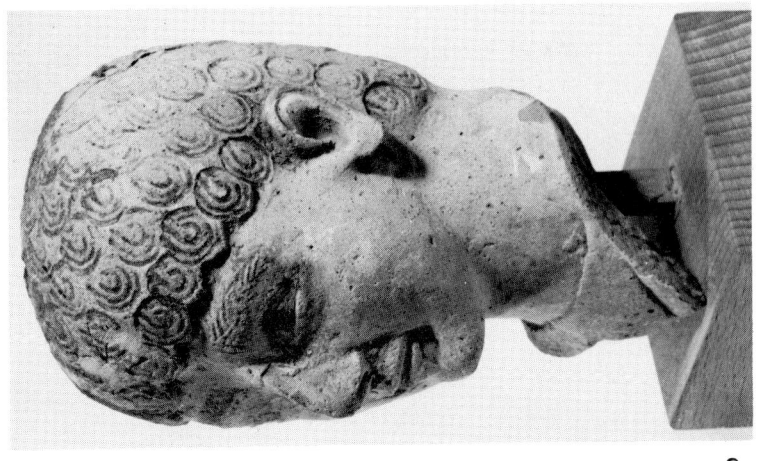

Plate XXIV: a. Terracotta head of a woman wearing jewellery. Cypro-Archaic. Given by L. Bowen. Ht. 0·14 [1926.551]. b. Terracotta head of a youth with short curly hair. Cypro-Archaic. From Salamis, given by the Cyprus Exploration Fund. Ht. 0·13 [1891.475].

imported to Cyprus points to the same development (pl. XXVI). The Greek link seems to have been strongest at Marium (modern Polis-tis-Khrysokhou), but similar evidence has been found at Salamis, Kition and Amathus. Cyprus, no doubt, produced copper for the west, as well as providing an invaluable entrepôt for Greek trade with the rich territories further east.

In the last years of the sixth century BC and the beginning of the fifth, Cyprus, to her great disadvantage, was drawn into a struggle for power between Greece and Persia which ebbed and flowed for the next 250 years. For the Greeks, control over Cyprus would have virtually ensured naval domination of the East Mediterranean and the consequent neutralising of the fleets of Persia and her allies (particularly Phoenicia). The history of Cyprus over this period is an index of the many vicissitudes through which this struggle was to pass. In 499 BC, Onesilus King of Salamis persuaded all his brother kings (except Amathus) to join the Greek cities of Ionia in their revolt against Persia. As a result, the Persians sent a powerful naval and military expedition to Cyprus and the Cypriots were heavily defeated in a land battle. A few months after that defeat the last city to resist, Soloi, had been reduced and the whole island passed under Persian rule. At Kouklia (Palaeopaphos) excavation has revealed the remains of a siege mound erected in 498 BC by the Persians by the north-west gate of the city; in the debris were found many fragmentary sculptures and dedications from some extramural sanctuary overrun by the besiegers. The results of this debâcle were seen a generation later when a flotilla of 150 Cypriot ships fought with the Persian fleet against the Greeks at the famous naval battle off the Greek island of Salamis in 480 BC. From what the ancient sources say, the hearts of the Cypriot sailors were not in the fight.

## THE CYPRO-CLASSIC PERIOD

After the Persians had been defeated in Greece on land and sea in 480 and 479 BC, and withdrew, the Athenians made a great effort to reduce Cyprus and deny it to the Persian King. A particularly determined attempt was made by an expedition led by Cimon. At least three of the strongest cities—Marium, Kition and Salamis—offered resistance. Marium was captured, but Kition was still under siege when Cimon died (probably of the pestilence that was rife in his fleet). In the face of this reverse the Greeks raised the siege and

# THE IRON AGE

Plate XXV: a. Salamis. Silver stater. Obverse, ram and uncertain royal name. Reverse, syllabic signs, 'of the king'. *c.* 460 BC. b. Kition. Silver stater of King Azbaal. Obverse, Heracles. Reverse, lion and stag, inscribed with the king's name in Phoenician. Third quarter of the 5th century BC. c. Salamis. Silver stater of Evagoras I. Obverse, Heracles. Reverse, goat, grain of corn above, inscribed with the king's name in Greek and the Cypriot syllabic script. 411-374/3 BC. (Enlarged.)

Plate XXVI: Attic Red-Figure lekythos by the Achilles Painter, Aphrodite riding on a swan *c.* 440 BC. From Polis tis Khrysokhou (Marium), Western Necropolis, Tomb 57, given by the Cyprus Exploration Fund. Ht. 0·310 [1891.451].

returned to the west, leaving Cyprus, at least for the time, under Persian control. But, although the throne of Salamis passed at this time to a Phoenician usurper, and Idalion (apparently Hellenised) was conquered and absorbed by Phoenician Kition, trade links with Greece persisted; during the second half of the fifth century BC some fine Athenian red-figure vases reached Marium (note the lekythos showing Aphrodite riding over the waves on a swan, attributed by Beazley to the Achilles Painter, pl. XXVI). In 411 BC the Phoenician interlude at Salamis was brought to an end by Evagoras I, a member of the ancient family of Teucrid kings of the

Plate XXVII: Limestone inscription in undeciphered Eteo-Cypriot. 4th century BC. Perhaps from a tomb at Polemidhia, Limassol, given by J. L. Myres. L. 0·68 [Inscription no. 119].

city, who quickly and deservedly won a reputation as a friend of Greece. For nearly 40 years he dominated Cypriot politics and played a considerable role in international affairs. The Athenians, indeed, were sufficiently grateful for his help after their sea-victory over the Spartans at Cnidus to erect a bronze statue to him in front of the Stoa Basileios in the market place in Athens.

Evagoras was successful in subjecting all the Cypriot cities to his authority. For the rest of his reign he was involved in a struggle with Persia, intent upon reasserting its authority in the East Mediterranean. His position was weakened after the Peace of Antalcidas in 386 BC, when Athens acknowledged the claim of the Persian king to the cities of Asia and the islands of Clazomenae and Cyprus. The Persians attacked Cyprus with determination and despite Evagoras' initial success eventually overwhelmed him. Even

Plate XXVIII: Bichrome Red ware jug with the mould-made figure of a woman carrying a jug on the shoulder. Cypro-Classic. From Polis tis Khrysokhou (Marium), Kaparga, Tomb 37, given by the Cyprus Exploration Fund. Ht. 0·274 [1890.690].

so, he contrived to negotiate a settlement with the Persians that left him in control of Salamis. He was required to pay tribute, yet seemed to treat the Persian king as an equal. He minted his own coinage in silver and gold inscribed with his name in both Greek and the Cypriot syllabic script (pl. XXVc). He concluded peace in 380 BC, but was murdered six or seven years later. His successors were lesser men, who continued an uneasy relationship with

Plate XXIX: Gold earring with bull-head finial. Hellenistic. D. 0·039 [1942.210]. (Enlarged.)

Persia. By 330 BC Persian domination had been removed for ever in the wake of the victories of Alexander the Great.

The years from the battle of Salamis in 480 BC until the death of Alexander in 323 were, as we have seen, turbulent ones for Cyprus. Little evidence of this turbulence appears in what has been recovered of contemporary material culture. The long established classes of decorated pottery developed in a largely unbroken sequence; White Painted ware was still popular, though its decoration grew increasingly slovenly. There was much less Bichrome pottery. Pl. XXVIII shows a characteristic jug of this period, of a type much liked at Marium, with an affix on the shoulder in the form of a kore (girl) with wine-jug. Other jugs had bull-head spouts (fig. IVa, 3). Almost certainly these are rather pedestrian copies of bronze jugs to which bronze statuettes of the wine-bearing girls were attached; none of these hypothetical metal vessels have survived. Some ceramic decoration—leaf-bands and palmettes in particular—were derived from Greek ornament, and serve as a further reminder of Greek influence. Jewellery and metalwork show Persian influence, exemplified by the so-called treasure from Vouni Palace, a Persian-type building set on a coastal hill-top dominating Soloi. Throughout the Hellenistic period into Roman times a particularly attractive type of earring was fashionable, with animal-head terminals—lions, bulls (pl. XXIX), goats, gazelles and, later, dolphins. Many were picked out with filigree-work (pl. XXIX); the hoops were made of twisted or plaited wire; sometimes beads of glass or hard stone were threaded on the hoops.

# IV. Hellenistic And Roman Cyprus

## THE HELLENISTIC PERIOD

Despite the notional freedom from Persian authority that resulted for the Cypriots, the conquests of Alexander marked the end of independence for Cyprus for centuries to come. After Alexander's death in 323 BC, Cyprus became involved in the struggles of his Successors, eventually falling to the share of Ptolemy I of Egypt and those who followed him. This was the end of the little city-states and their kings. Nikokreon, the last king of Salamis, fell foul of Ptolemy I and was forced into suicide; at the instigation of Nikokreon's wife, Axiothea, the whole royal family followed his example, firing the royal palace as they did so in a final gesture of defiance. A very remarkable burial mound was excavated near Salamis by Dr. Karageorghis in 1965 and 1966 which has been very convincingly identified as the cenotaph of this royal household. The mound had been raised over a platform built of mud-bricks on which had been a pyre; surrounding it, still on the platform, a number of life-size human figures modelled in clay had been set up on wooden posts. These figures may have represented the royal suicides, whose bodies could not be recovered for more normal burial. The ceremony at the pyre on the platform would thus have been a symbolic re-enactment of their end, and at the same time a funeral ceremony designed to ensure their passage to the underworld. This event took place in 311 or 310 BC. For the two-and-a-half centuries that followed, Cyprus was part of the Ptolemaic kingdom, administered as a military command and governed by an official with the title of *strategos*.

Under the Ptolemies Cyprus lost nearly all that remained of its own distinctive character in material civilisation, and appears as a somewhat provincial version of the wider Hellenistic world. In sculpture, for instance, poor imitations of Greek work were common (for example, the tomb relief, pl. XXXa). Notice pottery, terracottas and jewellery on display from tombs of this period at *Tsambres* and *Aphendrika*, near Rizokarpaso (see fig. IVb, 1–5).

ANCIENT CYPRUS

CYPRO CLASSIC

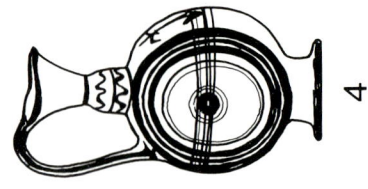
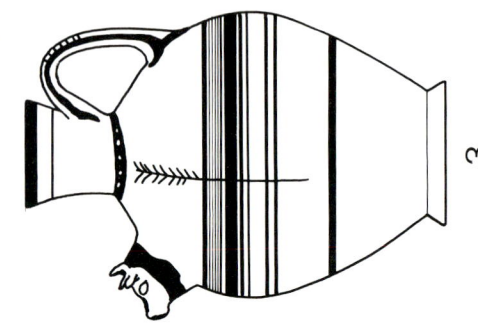
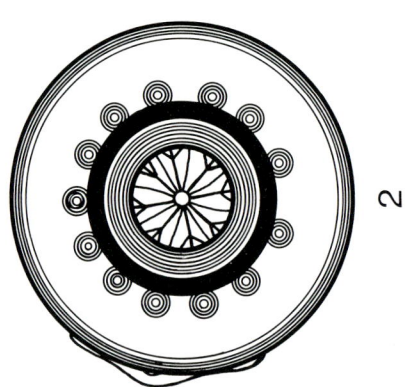
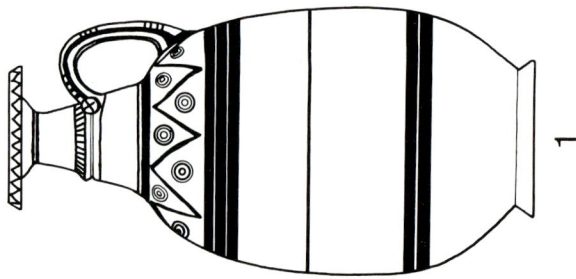

Black-on-Red ware
Fig. IVa

# HELLENISTIC AND ROMAN CYPRUS

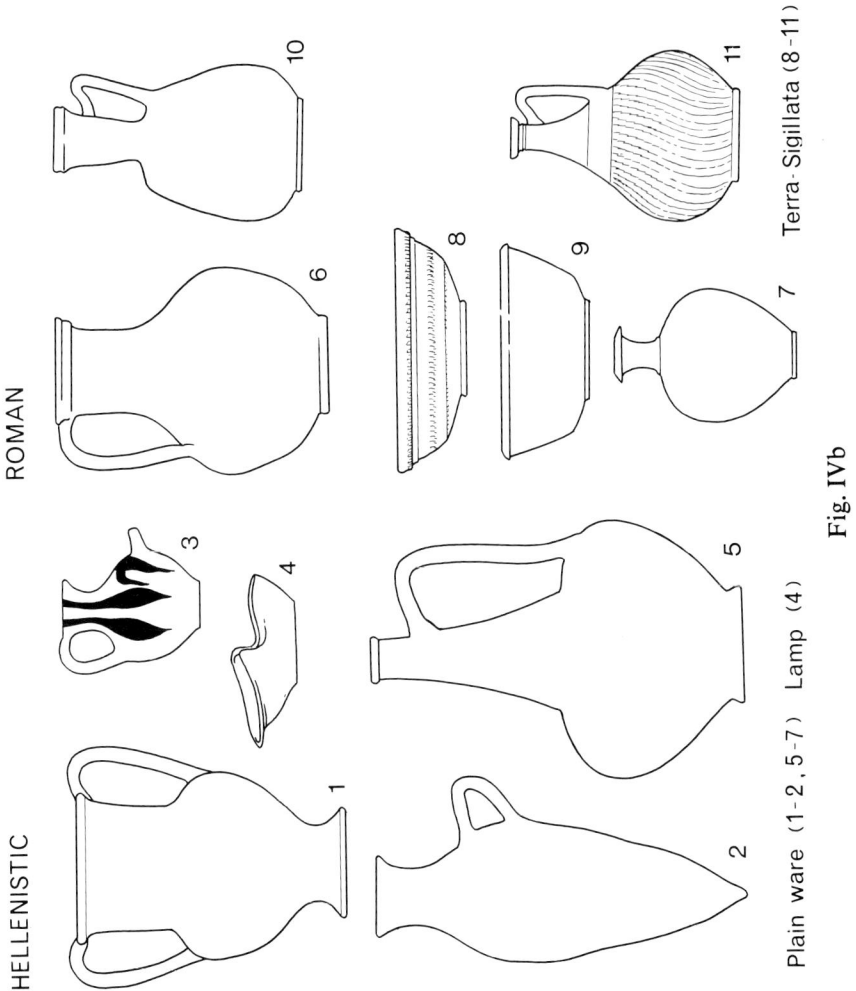

Fig. IVb

Plain ware (1-2, 5-7) Lamp (4) Terra-Sigillata (8-11)

One of the last traces of the old Cyprus is a series of dedications made during the late third century BC at the hill-shrine of a nymph at Kafizin, near Nicosia. Here, an official, Onesagoras, son of Philounios, offered pottery vessels inscribed, in many cases, in the old Cypriot syllabary. Some of his offerings were also inscribed in normal alphabetic Greek, and it is interesting that the Greek of the syllabic inscriptions is the old dialect of the island, Arcado-Cypriot, while the alphabetic inscriptions are straightforward Hellenistic Greek.

Cyprus must have been of considerable value to the Ptolemies; it was an important military base, as well as a useful source of copper, timber (particularly for ship-building) and grain. Archaeologically, the period has been relatively little explored, and is known chiefly from the investigations of sanctuaries and cemeteries. In many cases, subsequent Roman activity has largely covered or obliterated Hellenistic buildings, domestic or public, in the principal towns of Cyprus.

## THE ROMAN PERIOD

In 58 BC Cyprus was annexed by Rome, at the instigation of Publius Clodius Pulcher. The motive was expansionist, forming as it did an important step in the encirclement of Egypt. Its legality was extremely dubious, resting in large part on the alleged terms of a will supposed to have been made by the last legitimate Ptolemy. The incorruptible Marcus Porcius Cato was sent from Rome (where his absence was a great relief to his political opponents) to supervise the annexation, and the sale of the very substantial royal treasure of Cyprus. Cato eventually took back to Rome the huge sum of 7,000 talents as the proceeds of these transactions; the money was swallowed up in the Civil War.

The island was administered as a praetorian province, attached at first to Cilicia. There was a brief interval of resumed Egyptian dominance when, as part of the intrigue surrounding the Roman civil wars, Julius Caesar returned Cyprus to Ptolemaic Egypt. In 36 BC Marcus Antonius gave the island to Cleopatra as a present; on her death in 30 BC it reverted to Rome. From 22 BC onwards it was administered as a senatorial province, governed by a pro-Praetor with the title of Proconsul. On the reorganisation of the Empire under Diocletian, carried further by Constantine the Great,

Plate XXX: a. Limestone tomb relief, above a bearded banqueter with boy attendant, below a seated woman. Hellenistic. Given by John Ruskin. Ht. 1·83 [Michaelis 127]. b. Marble statue of Athena. Roman, first half of the 2nd century AD from the Gymnasium, Salamis. Given by the Cyprus Exploration Fund. Ht. 1·10 [1891.734].

a

Plate XXXI: a. Gold ring setting showing the Shrine of Aphrodite at Paphos. From the Nelidoff Collection. Ht. 0·022 [1931.548]. b. 'Cypriot sigillata' jug. Late 1st–2nd century AD. Given by T. Burton-Brown. Ht. 0·188 [1935.580]. c. Mould-made lamps. 1st century AD. Given by J. L. Myres. L. 0·085 [C.506] L. 0·084 [C.498].

b

c

Cyprus was allotted to the first of the twelve dioceses, that of the *Oriens*. When the Roman world was divided in AD 395, Cyprus, quite naturally, fell to the share of Byzantium.

The centuries of Roman rule were relatively calm and prosperous for the island, although we hear of occasional natural catastrophes, or rare political disasters. In 15 BC Nea Paphos was devastated by an earthquake; the Emperor Augustus came to the rescue with a gift for rebuilding and decreed that the city should be called Augusta. There were further severe earthquakes on the island, *c.* AD 75, and in the first half of the fourth century both Salamis and Nea Paphos were badly damaged. For Nea Paphos this was a blow from which the city never recovered; Salamis, granted exemption from taxes, was rebuilt and renamed Constantia, and became the most important city in the island. The most serious political unrest came in AD 116, when the Jewish troubles spread from Cyrene and Egypt to Cyprus. The Jews must have been an important element in the community. This is clearly illustrated in the *Acts*. Paul and Barnabas (the latter a native of Cyprus) landed at Salamis in AD 45 and travelled the length of the island preaching in the synagogues; at Nea Paphos they achieved the distinction of converting the proconsul, Sergius Paulus, despite (or because of) the intervention of his attendant, the magician Bar-jesus, who was struck blind.

Important buildings of the Roman period have been excavated and studied at Salamis, Soloi, Curium and Nea Paphos. At the latter, a particularly fine house, the so-called House of Dionysos, of the third century AD, has recently been excavated. Many of its rooms are paved with elaborate mosaics. One shows Dionysos and his retinue, another the god bestowing the gift of wine on Ikarios. Another pavement has a hunting scene with many different animals, including moufflon, the wild horned sheep of Cyprus, of which a few still survive in the mountainous areas of the Paphos Forest. Among important public buildings so far investigated is a Gymnasium at Salamis, from which came many marble sculptures, chiefly Roman copies of Classical and Hellenistic originals. A marble figure of Athena from the Cyprus Exploration Fund excavations of 1890 is in the Ashmolean (pl. XXXb, Randolph Gallery). Nea Paphos was the capital city of the province until the fourth century; Palaeopaphos some miles further east (modern Kouklia) was the centre of a very important cult of Aphrodite. Very little remains of the famous temple of the goddess; the best guide to its appearance is a representation of it that appears on some Cypriot coins of the Roman Empire, and, very rarely, on gold ring settings (pl. XXXIa). These show a three-room building, a cone-shaped aniconic cult-image and a courtyard.

When we turn to the minor items of material culture in Cyprus in the Roman period we find virtually nothing that is specifically Cypriot. Whatever it may be—sculpture, bronzes, jewellery, glass or pottery—the designs are familiar throughout much of the Roman world. Prototypes will have been imported and widely imitated by Cypriot manufacturers and craftsmen. Fine pottery for the table, the red *terra-sigillata*, made most successfully by potteries at Arezzo in Italy, was enthusiastically copied by Cypriot potters, who developed their own favourite shapes (pl. XXXIb, fig. IVb, 8–11). Coarser pottery was used for general household and kitchen purposes. Terracotta lamps were imported, many from the best factories in Italy, and then copied often in moulds that had been made directly from the imported pieces (pl. XXXIc). Much glass table-ware was sent from factories in Syria, and was also imitated in Cypriot workshops. For many purposes it replaced fine pottery and became a popular tomb offering.

# V. Early Christian, Byzantine, Medieval And Later Cyprus

## EARLY CHRISTIAN AND BYZANTINE CYPRUS

When at the end of the fourth century AD Cyprus became a part of the Eastern empire, it entered a period of two centuries of relatively peaceful existence as a rather neglected outpost. Perhaps the most significant episode in this period was the successful struggle of the Cypriot Church for independence from Antioch. The arguments both for and against independence were wide-ranging, and matters came to a head in the reign of Zeno, when it was claimed on one hand that Cyprus was not an Apostolic foundation (Paul and Barnabas had been conveniently forgotten), and that therefore the Church should be subject to Antioch, which undoubtedly was Apostolic. The outlook for an independent Cyprus was poor when, most happily, St. Barnabas himself appeared in a vision to the Archbishop Anthemius, directing him to the tomb where his remains were buried. On the saint's chest, where it had been placed by St. Mark, was the copy of the Gospel of St. Matthew, written by Barnabas himself. This compelling evidence of Apostolic foundation was taken by Anthemius to Constantinople. The Gospel was presented to the Emperor and not long after, the independence of the Church of Cyprus was formally recognised.

Although heavily taxed Cyprus enjoyed one of the greatest periods of prosperity in its history from the fifth to the seventh centuries AD. It was a time of church-building on a large scale, both in the chief towns and in more humble settlements. Several Early Christian basilican churches have been excavated—two at Salamis, others at Amathus, Curium, Peyia, Soloi and Tremetousha. Two surviving wall mosaics (one of the sixth century at Lythrankomi, one of the seventh at Kiti) give tantalising glimpses of the standard of decoration. Some further insight into the wealth of the period comes from the 'treasure' found at the end of the last century at Lambousa (the site of the ancient city of Lapethus, on the north

Plate XXXII: Glass Goblet. *c.* 6th century AD. Given by Rugby School. Ht. 0.10 [1950.35].

coast). The finds (now divided between Nicosia, London and New York) include jewellery and a fine series of decorated silver plate whose control stamps imply an origin in Byzantium itself. At a much lower level, local craftsmen continued a prolific pottery production of table and domestic wares, drinking cups and dishes, wine amphorae and cooking pots; glass-factories mass-produced wine goblets (pl. XXXII), and lamps for church candelabra.

The later seventh and the eighth centuries A.D. was a dark period for Cyprus, when innumerable villages and farms were abandoned and their lands neglected. The settlements that did survive dwindled in size. It is customary to blame this state of affairs upon the struggle for power in the east Mediterranean between the Arabs and the Byzantines, but this was almost certainly not the only cause. It is more probable that physical factors, including periods of prolonged drought and the spread of pestilence, made a major contribution to the disappearance of much of the island's population. This is not to deny the damage caused by the Arabs. In AD 648 Muawiya, Emir of Syria, led a strong expedition against the island; Salamis/Constantia was taken by siege and sacked, and Arab Chronicles tell of the rich treasures captured. Part of the rest of the island was temporarily occupied and a tribute levied. Thereafter, sovereignty over Cyprus was intermittently contested between the Byzantine emperors and the Arab caliphs. In the late seventh century, the Emperor Justinian even tried the expedient of moving the Cypriots to a new settlement at Nova Justinianopolis, near Cyzicus, on the south coast of the Sea of Marmora. This venture lasted only a few years, and the displaced Cypriots were being returned to their homes by AD 700. Cyprus was only finally relieved from Arab attacks in the tenth century. The Emperor Nicephorus II Phocas inflicted a severe defeat on the Arabs in AD 965, and the island was restored to Byzantine rule.

Cyprus continued part of the Byzantine Empire for two centuries more. There was sufficient recovery from the earlier catastrophes for fine churches to be built and decorated. The island increasingly became an entrepôt for the pilgrims of Western Christendom on their way to visit the Holy Places in Palestine. One of these visitors was Erik the Good, king of Denmark, who died at Paphos in AD 1103. Many pilgrim ships called at Larnaka, and the more devout attempted the journey to the monastery of Stavrovouni, long before endowed by St. Helena with the cross of the Good Thief and a fragment of the True Cross.

## CYPRUS UNDER RICHARD I OF ENGLAND AND THE LUSIGNAN DYNASTY

In AD 1184, Isaac Comnenus, great-nephew of the Emperor Manuel I, arrived in Cyprus with forged documents appointing him governor of the island. He assumed the Imperial diadem, and called himself the Holy Emperor of Cyprus, which he ruled as a tyrant for 7 years. He was overthrown by Richard I, Lionheart, King of England, on his way to the Third Crusade, in AD 1191. In company with Richard, but aboard a separate ship, were his sister Joanna of Sicily, and his betrothed Berengaria of Navarre. Richard's fleet was dispersed in a storm; some of the ships were wrecked off the coast of Cyprus, and the survivors who reached land were roughly handled at Isaac's instigation. Berengaria's ship was driven into Limassol, where Isaac tried to persuade the women to land, hoping to take them captive. On their refusal, the ship was denied all amenities, including water. Unfortunately for Isaac, Richard Lionheart with the rest of the fleet arrived at this point, landed, and forced Isaac to capitulate to him. Richard took possession of the island, and was married to Berengaria in the Chapel of St. George at Limassol, where she was also crowned Queen of England. Richard then continued to Acre and sold Cyprus to the Knights Templar, who were not long in discovering that they were unable to hold the island by force. In turn, then, the island was offered to Guy de Lusignan, former king of the Frankish Kingdom of Jerusalem who had lost his throne on the capture of Jerusalem by Saladin in 1187.

It was left to Guy's brother and successor, Aimery, to take the title of King of Cyprus for the first time, in 1196. From that date, until AD 1498, the island was ruled by this Frankish Lusignan dynasty and, at court level, enjoyed a brilliant and prosperous time. The island derived a particular importance from its proximity to the Holy Land, first as a base for continuing crusade activity until the fall of Acre in 1291, later as a base for trade with the lands in Moslem hands. For the Cypriots themselves the period was not a happy one, and there was relatively little intermixing between them and their feudal lords and the Western merchants who established themselves particularly at the key port town of Famagusta, a few miles south of the now abandoned site of Salamis/Constantia. This division between the rulers and the ruled was exacerbated by the rift between the Latin Church and the Orthodox Church. The latter was relegated to a very subordinate position.

Many of the most imposing standing monuments in Cyprus are the product of the Lusignan period, including the castles of the Kyrenia Mountains—St. Hilarion, Buffavento and Kantara (all on earlier Byzantine foundations) and the Latin Cathedrals of Nicosia (Santa Sophia) and Famagusta (St. Nicholas). The

Plate XXXIII: Base gold bezant of Henry I, king of Cyprus. Reverse, the standing figure of the king with vestments and regalia in Byzantine style. Inscription HENRICUS REX CIPRI. AD. 1218–1253. (Enlarged.)

Premonstratensian Abbey of Bellapais, on the seaward foothills of the Kyrenia mountains, is one of the finest monuments of the Latin East. In the Ashmolean, this period in the history of Cyprus is illustrated by pottery and coins. The pottery represented is the attractive glazed *sgraffito* ware that was used throughout the island. Some of the finest bowls were made in the fourteenth century; though the ornament is frequently linear, some are decorated with the figures of knights in Western dress (pl. XXXIV), birds, shields of arms and other devices. Much of this pottery has been recovered from graves. The coins show first the Byzantine style of court dress (pl. XXXIII) and later various aspects of Western feudalism and heraldry (pl. XXXV).

Plate XXXIV: Brown and green *sgraffito* bowl. 14th century AD. Warrior carrying sword and shield. From Elea, J. Brew loan. D. 0·155.

## CYPRUS UNDER THE VENETIANS AND TURKS

From the beginning of the fourteenth century Venice and Genoa, the great Mediterranean trading nations of the Middle Ages, had established very powerful and influential depots in Cyprus, particularly at Famagusta, to support their eastern trading interests. Their presence was to prove disastrous for the Lusignans. A very grave situation developed after the coronation of Peter II in Famagusta in 1372. On such solemn occasions a Venetian led the king's horse by the left rein, but a Genoese by the (more prestigious) right rein. On this occasion, the Venetian attempted to oust the Genoese from his rightful place, and fighting broke out. When peace was restored two years later it was at the price of Famagusta being ceded to Genoa. Genoa and Venice were in constant conflict thereafter, while the Lusignans suffered heavily from the loss of revenue. In the early fifteenth century matters deteriorated still further as a result of encouragement given by the King of Cyprus to pirates raiding the lands of the Sultan of Egypt from Cypriot ports. The Mamelukes responded in 1426 with a devastating assault on Cyprus, in which the Lusignan army was heavily defeated at the Battle of Khirokitia; King Janus was captured and taken to Cairo, and the victorious Mameluke army sacked Limassol and Nicosia. Janus was eventually ransomed, but Cyprus remained a tributary of Egypt, even after the Mamelukes were replaced by the Turks in 1517.

It was not long before Cyprus once more fell victim to East Mediterranean power politics. From 1432 to 1458, the King was John II, whose second wife, the Greek Helena Palaeologa, tried to alleviate the lot of the oppressed Orthodox Church. John and Helena had no male heirs, and this encouraged James the Bastard, natural son of John and a friend of Egypt and Venice, to make a successful bid for the throne (pl. XXXVc). The Venetians, with prescience, provided James with a Venetian wife, Katerina Cornaro. Their son, James III, the last King of Cyprus, was born after his father's death, but died as a small baby. For a while his mother was allowed nominal sovereignty, but in 1489 Venice annexed the island, and attempted to turn it into a forward defence area against the growing threat of the Osmanli Turks. Nicosia, Kyrenia and Famagusta were refortified; in the case of Nicosia, the old Medieval

# ANCIENT CYPRUS

Plate XXXV: a. Silver gros of Amaury de Lusignan, Prince of Tyre (usurper), Governor of the Kingdom of Jerusalem and Cyprus. Reverse, the arms of Jerusalem and Lusignan. Inscription IRL'M ET CIPRI REGIS FILIUS. AD. 1306–1310. b. Silver gros of Peter I king of Jerusalem and Cyprus. Obverse, the king seated on his throne, his shield beside him. Inscription PIERE PAR LA GRACE DE DIE ROI. AD. 1359–1369. c. Silver gros of James II the Bastard. Obverse, the king on horseback carrying a sword. Inscription IACOBO DEI GR. AD 1460–1473. (Enlarged.)

78

capital was largely demolished in order to build the present walled city to the design of Ascanio Savorgnano, the Venetian engineer. In 1570, on the direction of the Sultan Selim II, a Turkish force under Lala Mustafa Pasha landed near Limassol and, advancing on Nicosia, captured it after a 7-week siege. Famagusta held out for nearly a year longer, under the command of the *proveditore* Marc Antonio Bragadino, who was brutally murdered after the surrender.

From 1571 Cyprus became part of the Ottoman Empire; the Cypriots once more had exchanged one foreign government for another, though their condition under the Turks, initially at least, was probably an improvement on Venetian rule. The Orthodox Church recovered a good deal of its former eminence, and its Archbishops attained a position of political as well as spiritual importance. The Latin Church, by contrast, was eliminated, and the cathedrals of Nicosia and Famagusta became and remain the chief mosques in the island. In 1878 Turkey ceded the administration of Cyprus *de facto*, if not *de jure*, to Great Britain, who assumed full sovereignty in 1914 on the entry of Turkey into the Great War on the side of Britain's enemies. Cyprus became an independent state within the Commonwealth in 1960.

# Select Bibliography

## GENERAL

S. Casson, *Ancient Cyprus*, London, 1937.

L. P. di Cesnola, *Cyprus, its Ancient Cities, Tombs and Temples*, London, 1877.

R. Gunnis, *Historic Cyprus* (2nd ed.), London, 1947.

Sir George Hill, *A History of Cyprus*, vols. I–III, Cambridge, 1940–1948.

G. Jeffery, *Historic Monuments of Cyprus*, Nicosia, 1918.

V. Karageorghis, *The Ancient Civilisation of Cyprus*, London, 1970.

E. Oberhummer, *Die Insel Cypern*, Munich, 1903.

## CYPRIOT PREHISTORY—NEOLITHIC AND BRONZE AGE

P. Aström, *The Middle Cypriote Bronze Age*, Lund, 1972; *Swedish Cyprus Expedition*, IV, pt. 1b; *The Late Cypriote Bronze Age: Architecture and Pottery*, Lund, 1972; *Swedish Cyprus Expedition*, IV, pt. 1c.

P. and L. Aström, *The Late Cypriote Bronze Age; Other Arts and Crafts: Chronology, etc.*, Lund, 1972; *Swedish Cyprus Expedition*, IV, pt. 1d.

H.-G. Buchholz and V. Karageorghis, *Prehistoric Greece and Cyprus*, London, 1973.

H. W. Catling, 'Cyprus in the Neolithic and Bronze Age Periods' (Cambridge, 1966), Fasc. of revised edition of the *Cambridge Ancient History*.

P. Dikaios and J. R. Stewart, *The Stone Age and the Early Bronze Age in Cyprus*, Lund, 1962; *Swedish Cyprus Expedition*, IV, pt. Ia.

## CYPRUS IN THE IRON AGE—GEOMETRIC, ARCHAIC AND CLASSICAL

E. Gjerstad, *The Cypro-Geometric, Cypro-Archaic and Cypro-*

SELECT BIBLIOGRAPHY

*Classical Periods*, Stockholm, 1948; *Swedish Cyprus Expedition*, IV, pt. 2.

V. Karageorghis, *Excavations in the Necropolis of Salamis*, I, II and III, Nicosia, 1967, 1970 and 1973.

K. Spyridakis, *Euagoras I von Salamis*, Stuttgart, 1935.

## HELLENISTIC AND ROMAN CYPRUS

V. Karageorghis and C. C. Vermeule, *Sculptures from Salamis* I and II, Nicosia, 1964, 1966.

O. Vessberg and A. Westholm, *The Hellenistic and Roman Periods in Cyprus*, Stockholm, 1956; *Swedish Cyprus Expedition*, IV, pt. 3.

## BYZANTINE CYPRUS

A. Papageorghiou, *Masterpieces of the Byzantine Art of Cyprus*, Nicosia, 1965.

P. A. Soteriou, *Ta Byzantina Mnemeia tis Kyprou*, Athens, 1935.

A. and J. A. Stylianou, *Byzantine Cyprus*, Nicosia, 1948.

## CYPRUS UNDER THE FRANKS, AND LATER

C. D. Cobham, *Excerpta Cypria*, Cambridge, 1908.

C. Enlart, *L'Art Gothique et la Renaissance en Chypre*, Paris, 1899.

J. Hackett, *The Church of Cyprus*, London, 1901.

Sir George Hill, *A History of Cyprus*, II and III, Cambridge 1948. The same, vol. IV, edited Sir Harry Luke.

Sir Harry Luke, *Cyprus under the Turks*, London, 1921.

L. Machaeras, *Recital concerning the Sweet Land of Cyprus*. Translated and edited by R. M. Dawkins, Oxford, 1932.

## EPIGRAPHY

O. Masson, *Inscriptions Chypriotes Syllabiques*, Paris, 1961.

O. Masson and M. Sznycer, *Recherches sur les Phéniciens à Chypre*, Paris, 1972.

T. B. Mitford, *The Inscriptions of Kourion*, Philadelphia, 1971.

I. M.- Nikolaou, *Cypriot Inscribed Stones*, Nicosia, 1971.

## ART AND ARTIFACTS

H. W. Catling, *Cypriot Bronzework in the Mycenaean World*, Oxford, 1964.

T. J. Chamberlayne, *Lacrimae Nicossienses: Inscriptions Funeraires*, Paris, 1894.

Sir George Hill, *Catalogue of the Greek Coins of Cyprus in the British Museum*, London, 1904.

V. Karageorghis, *Treasures in the Cyprus Museum*, Nicosia, 1962; *Corpus Vasorum Antiquorum: Cyprus*, Fascs. 1 and 2, Nicosia, 1963, 1965.

A. Pieridou, *Jewellery in the Cyprus Museum*, Nicosia, 1971.

## MUSEUM GUIDES AND COLLECTIONS

P. Dikaios, *A Guide to the Cyprus Museum*, 3rd ed. revised, Nicosia, 1961.

V. Karageorghis, *Cypriote Antiquities in the Pierides Collection*. Published privately in Cyprus, 1973.

J. L. Myres, *Handbook of the Cesnola Collection of Antiquities from Cyprus*, New York, 1914.

J. R. Stewart, in *Handbook to the Nicholson Museum* (2nd ed.), Sydney, 1948.

Preliminary reports of new excavations or discoveries are made annually in the *Report of the Department of Antiquities, Cyprus (RDAC)*, in the *Annual Report of the Director of Antiquities, Cyprus (ARDA*—since 1949) and in 'Chronique des Fouilles et Découvertes Archéologiques à Chypre' published in *Bulletin de Correspondance Hellénique* since 1959. More summary accounts at longer intervals in *Archaeological Reports, American Journal of Archaeology* and *Archäologischer Anzeiger*.

# Index of Excavated Material from Cyprus in the Ashmolean Museum

NOTE. Some tomb groups are shared with other Museums. Certain material originally in Oxford has been transferred to other collections. The following abbreviations are used:

*JHS*    Journal of Hellenic Studies
*RDAC* Report of the Department of Antiquities, Cyprus

1888. Cyprus Exploration Fund (including D. G. Hogarth, Keeper of the Ashmolean 1909–1927).

*Nicosia District*
    *Eylenja—Leontari Vouno*, Middle Cypriot Tombs, *JHS* IX, 152 ff.

*Paphos District*
    *Kouklia (Palaeopaphos)*, Tomb 2 (Late Cypriot IIIB); Later tombs; Temple of Aphrodite (Hellenistic and Roman), *JHS* IX, 158 ff.
    *Amargetti*, Sanctuary of Opaon Melanthios (Hellenistic and Roman), *JHS* IX, 171 ff.

1888–1890. Cyprus Exploration Fund (under H. A. Tubbs, Pembroke College, J. A. R. Munro (later Rector of Lincoln College) and E. A. Gardner, Director of the British School at Athens).

*Nicosia District*
    *Limniti*, Archaic Sanctuary Site, *JHS* XI, 82 ff.

*Paphos District*
    *Polis-tis-Khrysokhou (Marium)*, Archaic, Classical and Hellenistic tombs.
    Sites A, K, B, M; Ayios Dimitrios Tomb 10; Oven Site Tombs B, E, L; *JHS* XI, 1 ff. Western Necropolis Tombs 57, 67, *JHS* XII, 298 ff.

*Famagusta District*

*Salamis*, Archaic sanctuary at Toumba; Sites E and F (Archaic-Roman); Gymnasium (Hellenistic-Roman), *JHS* XII, 95 ff.

1894. British School at Athens (J. L. Myres), with residue of Cyprus Exploration Fund.

*Nicosia District*

*Nicosia–Ayia Paraskevi*, Early and Middle Cypriot tombs, *JHS* XVII, 134–138.

*Famagusta District*

*Kalopsidha*, Early and Middle Cypriot Settlement; Early and Middle Cypriot Tombs 2, 8–11, 13, 19–21, 26–27, *JHS* XVII, 138–147.

*Larnaka District*

Sites associated with ancient Kition (modern Larnaka).
*Batsalos*, Classical sanctuary, *JHS* XVII, 170–171.
*Hassan Effendi*, Archaic cemetery, tombs 4 and 7, *JHS* XVII, 153.
*Kamelarga*, Archaic sanctuary, *JHS* XVII, 164–169.
*Laxia tou Riou*, Late Cypriot cemetery, tombs 1 and 4, *JHS* XVII, 147–152.

*Turabi Tekke*, Archaic cemetery, tombs 6, 15, 20, 28, 44, 55–56, 60, *JHS* XVII, 152–164.

1933–1935. Cyprus Museum (P. Dikaios). Set of specimen material sent to Oxford.

*Limassol District*

*Erimi*, Chalcolithic settlement, *RDAC* 1936, 5 ff.

1937–1938. British School at Athens (J. R. Stewart).

*Kyrenia District*

*Bellapais-Vounous*, Early Cypriot cemetery, tombs 92, 131A, 132 and 161 (Part Birmingham loan) E. and J. R. Stewart, *Vounous*, 1937–1938, Lund, 1950.

1938. Ashmolean Museum and Department of Antiquities, Cyprus (J. du Plat Taylor).

*Famagusta District*
   *Rizokarpaso–Tsambres*, Late Classical and Hellenistic cemetery, tombs 1, 10, 12, 15, 16 and 18.
   *Rizokarpaso–Aphendrika*, Late Classical and Hellenistic cemetery, tombs 33, 36–37, 46, 48. *RDAC* 1937–1939, 24 ff.

1949. Mission Archéologique Française (C. F. A. Schaeffer).

*Famagusta District*
   *Enkomi*, Late Cypriot cemetery, tombs 5 and 11 (Specimens. C.F.A. Schaeffer, *Enkomi–Alasia*, Paris, 1952).

1950–1951. Ashmolean Museum—Sydney University Expedition (J. du Plat Taylor).

*Kyrenia District*
   *Myrtou–Pigadhes*, Late Cypriot settlement and sanctuary; Geometric sanctuary, J. du Plat Taylor, *Myrtou-Pigadhes*, Oxford, 1957.

1955. University of Melbourne Expedition (J. R. Stewart), with Ashmolean subvention.

*Kyrenia District*
   *Vasilia*, Early Cypriot cemetery, tomb 1 (dromos group).

1971. University of Birmingham (E. J. Peltenburg), with Ashmolean subvention.

*Kyrenia District*
   *Ayios Epiktitos–Vrysi*, Neolithic settlement, *RDAC* 1972, 1 ff.